The KGB and the Stasi: The History of the East's Intelligence Agencies

By Charles River Editors

The KGB's emblem

About Charles River Editors

Charles River Editors is a boutique digital publishing company, specializing in bringing history back to life with educational and engaging books on a wide range of topics. Keep up to date with our new and free offerings with this 5 second sign up on our weekly mailing list, and visit Our Kindle Author Page to see other recently published Kindle titles.

We make these books for you and always want to know our readers' opinions, so we encourage you to leave reviews and look forward to publishing new and exciting titles each week.

Introduction

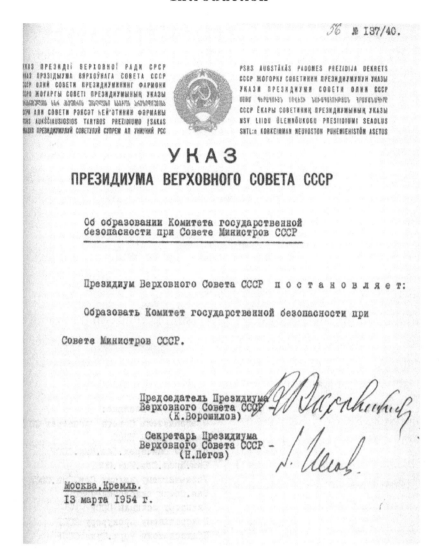

The document establishing the KGB

The KGB

"[T]he Stasi often used a method which was really diabolic. It was called Zersetzung, and it's described in another guideline. The word is difficult to translate because it means originally "biodegradation". But actually, it's a quite accurate description. The goal was to destroy secretly the self-confidence of people, for example by damaging their reputation, by organizing failures in their work, and by destroying their personal relationships. Considering this, East Germany was a very modern dictatorship. The Stasi didn't try to arrest every dissident. It preferred to paralyze them, and it could do so because it had access to so much personal information and to so many institutions." - Hubertus Knabe, German historian

The KGB is one of the most famous abbreviations of the 20th century, and it has become synonymous with the shadowy and often violent actions of the Soviet Union's secret police and internal security agencies. In fact, it is often used to refer to the Soviet state security agencies throughout its history, from the inception of the inception of the Cheka (Extraordinary Commission) in 1917 to the official elimination of the KGB in 1992. Whether it's associated with the Russian Civil War's excesses, Stalin's purges, and even Vladimir Putin, the KGB has long been viewed as the West's biggest bogeyman during the second half of the 20th century.

Aside from the KGB, the 20th century's most notorious spy agency was the Stasi, which was instrumental in the history of East Germany. In an era of totalitarian countries dominated by repressive state agencies, the Stasi stood out for its size, and the sheer breadth and depth of its surveillance. Films such as *Das Leben der Anderen* ("The Lives of Others") encapsulated post-unification attitudes and conceptions of both life in East Germany and the activities of the Stasi.

Despite its notoriety, the legacy of the Stasi is contested in modern Germany. Former West Germans, and Westerners more generally, closely align the East German state and the Stasi, framing a "Stasi State." Those in the former East Germany, however, resent the patronizing attitudes and conflation of the two institutions, preferring to focus on the social elements of the East German state. Uwe Spiekermann, of the German Historical Institute, succinctly sets out the impressions of many when considering East Germany and its culture of surveillance: "In retrospect, the Stasi has become a symbol for the GDR [East Germany]."

The East German State Security Service, or Staatssicherheitsdienst in German (abbreviated to Stasi) was formed in 1950. It purported to be the state's "shield and sword" and closely monitored much of the population for the next 40 years. Some of the figures are startling. By the end of the 1980s, Stasi files were kept on six million out of 18 million inhabitants. When the Stasi archives were opened in the 1990s, files were discovered that stretched for 178 kilometers. Over the course of East Germany's existence, up to two million people acted as spies, and 90,000 people worked at the Ministry, not to mention the numerous "unofficial" informers.

East Germany also had a much-feared foreign intelligence arm of its intelligence services, the HV A (German: Hauptverwaltung A or central department), which proved expert at infiltrating West German society and running operations in numerous other countries. But why did the Stasi form, and how did it prove so effective? Answering those questions requires understanding the unique circumstances in which East Germany was formed, as well as politics in Germany at the end of World War II and the start of the Cold War.

The KGB and the Stasi: The History of the Eastern Bloc's Most Infamous Intelligence Agencies examines two notorious agencies. Along with pictures depicting important people, places, and events, you will learn about the KGB and Stasi like never before.

The KGB and the Stasi: The History of the Eastern Bloc's Most Infamous Intelligence Agencies

About Charles River Editors

Introduction

    The Russian Revolution and the Formation of the Cheka

    Reorganizing the Cheka

    Stalin and Spying

    The Birth of East Germany

    The Birth of the Stasi

    The Formation of the KGB

    Suppressing the 1953 Uprising in East Germany

    Erich Mielke and Markus Wolf

    Strengthening the KGB

    High Socialism and Supreme Control

    The Guillaume Scandal

    The Stasi and Daily Life

    Elimination

    The End of the Stasi

    Online Resources

    Further Reading about the KGB

    Further Reading about the Stasi

Free Books by Charles River Editors

Discounted Books by Charles River Editors

The Russian Revolution and the Formation of the Cheka

Vladimir Lenin's plan for a Russian Civil War received a catalyst from a strange place. In September of 1915, Tsar Nicholas II dismissed his generals on the Eastern Front during World War I and took over military command himself. Thus, as the number of battles lost grew, his reputation and popularity among the people fell. By 1917, it was clear that the Russian Army would never be able to sustain further involvement in the war, having already lost almost 8 million soldiers to death, injury and capture. With that, the Russian people began to cry out against the privations of the war. Factory workers staged strikes for higher wages to pay the ever inflating cost of food for their families. At the same time, people in Petrograd rioted in the streets, vandalizing shops and demanding food that the government simply did not have.

Lenin

Had he been wiser, Nicholas might have appealed to the people, or met with the Duma to work out some sort of solution to the shortages. However, he had been raised with the understanding that the main work of a Tsar was to preserve the monarchy for his son. Thus, he decided on the very inopportune moment of late February, 1917 to try to disband the Duma and regain absolute power. When the Duma refused to disband, the High Commander of the army appealed to Nicholas, suggesting that he should abdicate before a full scale revolution broke out. Some suggested that the Tsar's cousin, Grand Duke Michael Alexandrovich would make an excellent replacement. He refused, however, and on March 1, Nicholas was forced to leave and was replaced with a Provisional Government which originally consisted of a mishmash of parliamentary figures and members of revolutionary councils that had been elected by workers, soldiers and peasants.

Lenin was still in exile in Zurich when the February Revolution pushed Nicholas II out of power, and he only found out about it on March 15. Understandably thrilled with this turn of events, Lenin began firing off missives to friends and allies in an attempt to harness the revolutionary energy and direct it toward an international class conflict, writing in one letter, "Spread out! Rouse new sections! Awaken fresh initiative, form new organisations in every stratum and prove to them that peace can come only with the armed Soviet of Workers' Deputies in power." At the same time, he and other members of the Provisional Government went about trying to secure his safe passage back to Russia, and eventually a Swiss colleague with contacts in the German Foreign Ministry was able to get Lenin a train ride into Russia. While that seems odd at first glance, it is apparent the German Foreign Ministry hoped that Lenin's agitation back in Russia would sufficiently distract the Russian Army and lead to their surrender to Germany or their quitting of the war.

The locomotive that brought Lenin back to Russia

Joining Lenin on his private train were 27 fellow Bolsheviks anxious to press forward the cause of socialism and shape the new political system. Passing through Germany, some passengers on the train were "struck by the total absence of grown-up men. Only women, teenagers and children could be seen at the wayside stations, on the fields, and in the streets of the towns." Lenin, however, was all about business. While on the train, he completed work on what became known as his famous April Theses, and he read them aloud as soon as he entered Petrograd on April 3rd. In it he outlined his plans for the immediate future:

1. In view of the undoubted honesty of the mass of rank and file representatives of revolutionary defencism who accept the war only as a necessity and not as a means of conquest,

in view of their being deceived by the bourgeoisie, it is necessary most thoroughly, persistently, patiently to explain to them their error, to explain the inseparable connection between capital and the imperialist war, to prove that without the overthrow of capital it is impossible to conclude the war with a really democratic, non-oppressive peace.

2. The peculiarity of the present situation in Russia is that it represents a transition from the first stage of the revolution - which, because of the inadequate organization and insufficient class-consciousness of the proletariat, led to the assumption of power by the bourgeoisie - to its second stage which is to place power in the hands of the proletariat and the poorest strata of the peasantry.

3. No support to the Provisional Government; exposure of the utter falsity of all its promises, particularly those relating to the renunciation of annexations. Unmasking, instead of admitting, the illusion-breeding "demand" that this government, a government of capitalist, should cease to be imperialistic.

4. Recognition of the fact that in most of the Soviets of Workers' Deputies our party constitutes a minority, and a small one at that, in the face of the bloc of all the petty bourgeois opportunist elements who have yielded to the influence of the bourgeoisie.

It must be explained to the masses that the Soviet of Workers' Deputies is the only possible form of revolutionary government and that, therefore, our task is, while this government is submitting to the influence of the bourgeoisie, to present a patient, systematic, and persistent analysis of its errors and tactics, an analysis especially adapted to the practical needs of the masses.

5. Not a parliamentary republic - a return to it from the Soviet of Workers' Deputies would be a step backward - but a republic of Soviets of Workers', Agricultural Labourers' and Peasants' Deputies throughout the land, from top to bottom.

Abolition of the police, the army, the bureaucracy. All officers to be elected and to be subject to recall at any time, their salaries not to exceed the average wage of a competent worker.

6. In the agrarian program, the emphasis must be shifted to the Soviets of Agricultural Laborers' Deputies [including]

a. Confiscation of private lands.

b. Nationalization of all lands in the country, and management of such lands by local Soviets of Agricultural Labourers' and Peasants' Deputies.

c. A separate organization of Soviets of Deputies of the poorest peasants.

    d.   Creation of model agricultural establishments out of large estates.

7.   Immediate merger of all the banks in the country into one general national bank, over which the Soviet of Workers' Deputies should have control.

8.   Not the "introduction" of Socialism as an immediate task, but the immediate placing of the Soviet of Workers' Deputies in control of social production and distribution of goods.

9.   Party tasks [include] Immediate calling of a party convention and Changing the party program, mainly:

    a.   Concerning imperialism and the imperialist war.

    b.   Concerning our attitude toward the state, and our demand for a 'commune state."

    c.   Amending our antiquated minimum program.

10.   Rebuilding the International. Taking the initiative in the creation of a revolutionary International, an International against the social-chauvinists and against the "center".

Although the turmoil had been limited to Russia so far, and the Theses were written about how to immediately create a socialist state in Russia, it's clear that Lenin envisioned an international revolution even at this early date. As one historian characterized his thinking in 1917, "Lenin made his revolution for the sake of Europe, not for the sake of Russia, and he expected Russia's preliminary revolution to be eclipsed when the international revolution took place. Lenin did not invent the iron curtain."

Lenin's April Theses were among the most radical writings of his life to date, and both Mensheviks and fellow Bolsheviks were taken aback. The Theses were roundly condemned by the Mensheviks (one of whom described them as the "ravings of a madman"), and initially the Theses were supported by only one prominent Bolshevik, Alexandra Kollontai.

Kollontai

One of the people that were concerned about Lenin's insistence on an immediate revolution was Joseph Stalin. While he had always been fascinated by Lenin's ideals, he was usually too pragmatic to begin a venture without an assurance of success. Stalin had been in exile himself until returning to Siberia, and by April 1917 he was the editor of the popular Bolshevik paper *Pravda*. Stalin could not remain silent forever. Though Stalin and other Bolsheviks still believed that the revolution should be a bourgeoise revolution, the Theses at least presented a party platform and a banner under which revolutionaries could rally and united. Thus, after wrestling with the issue for ten days, Stalin wrote a scathing article supporting Lenin and urging the peasants to rise up immediately. He further instructed them to begin by forming local committees that would confiscate large, privately owned estates and turn them over to the peasants that worked on them. Even still, Lenin was going in an ideologically different direction, one that brought him closer to the political leanings of Leon Trotsky.

Stalin

Trotsky's journey from New York to Russia was slowed by a last-ditch effort to keep him out of Russia by detaining him in Nova Scotia, but he arrived in May 1917. In the months that followed, he developed a closer relationships with the Bolsheviks, who at the time were a relatively weak and marginal player in the chaotic political scene. Soon after, he was arrested under orders from Kerensky, who distrusted him because of his fiery leadership of the Soviet and clear involvement in Bolshevik plots to seize power. However, Trotsky was not held long, and when he was released, his ferocious criticism of the Provisional Government was successful in swaying the urban workers and soldiers toward the Bolshevik position. He was about to become indispensable to Lenin.

Trotsky

   The chaos continued when Alexander Kerensky, the new head of the Provisional Government, launched yet another military offensive against the Germans in July of 1917. Soldiers deserted by the thousands, with many of them carrying their government issued weapons back to the estates where they lived. They often used these guns to threaten or even kill their landlords so that they could have their land. They also burned stately mansions and moved ancient boundary stones to create new, smaller farms for the peasants themselves to own.

Kerensky

Alarmed by the rioting and believing that it was a result of the impact Lenin and other revolutionaries were having on the common people, Kerensky outlawed the Bolsheviks and tried to round up its members, outlandishly accusing them of being German agents. Trotsky famously defended Lenin and other Bolsheviks against the charge, exhorting, "An intolerable atmosphere has been created, in which you, as well as we, are choking. They are throwing dirty accusations at Lenin and [Grigory] Zinoviev. Lenin has fought thirty years for the revolution. I have fought [for] twenty years against the oppression of the people. And we cannot but cherish a hatred for German militarism . . . I have been sentenced by a German court to eight months' imprisonment for my struggle against German militarism. This everybody knows. Let nobody in this hall say that we are hirelings of Germany." Luckily for Lenin, he got wind of the threat well enough ahead of time to escape to Finland, where he completed work on *State and Revolution*, an outline of the government he hoped to one day see in Russia.

Lenin in disguise in Finland, 1917

As the rioting was going on back at home, Kerensky's July Offensive failed miserably, and he came into conflict with his new general, Lavr Kornilov, over policies related to discipline and production. When Kornilov sent the troops under his command to march on Kerensky's headquarters in Petrograd, Kerensky had to appeal to the Bolsheviks for Red Guards to protect his capitol city. Lenin reluctantly agreed and immediately recruited more than 25,000 soldiers to protect the government he so vehemently opposed. When Kornilov's troops saw the rows of dug in Red Guards, they refused to advance, and Kornilov surrendered to the palace police.

Realizing that he now had the Provisional Government largely at his mercy, Lenin returned to Russia in October and set up a party headquarters in Smolny Institute for Girls in St. Petersburg. From there, he quietly ordered that the Provisional Government be deposed and the Winter Palace vacated. On the evening of October 25, the Second All-Russian Congress of Soviets met at the Smolny Institute to establish a new government. While there were initially some disagreements over the overthrow of the Provisional Government, Martov's Mensheviks and Lenin's Bolsheviks eventually agreed to share power. Ironically, after all the drama that had surrounded the earlier months of that year, the October Revolution went largely unnoticed. As Lenin had written a month earlier, "The peaceful development of any revolution is, generally speaking, extremely rare and difficult ... but ... a peaceful development of the revolution is possible and probable if all power is transferred to the Soviets. The struggle of parties for power within the Soviets may proceed peacefully, if the Soviets are made fully democratic." It seemed that way in October.

Lenin arrived at the meeting the next evening to thunderous applause, appearing without a disguise for the first time since July. Famous American journalist John Reed, who would later chronicle the Russian Revolution in his critically acclaimed book, *Ten Days That Shook The World*, described Lenin for readers. "A short, stocky figure, with a big head set down in his shoulders, bald and bulging. Little eyes, a snubbish nose, wide, generous mouth, and heavy chin; clean-shaven now, but already beginning to bristle with the well-known beard of his past and future. Dressed in shabby clothes, his trousers much too long for him. Unimpressive, to be the idol of a mob, loved and revered as perhaps few leaders in history have been. A strange popular leader—a leader purely by virtue of intellect; colourless, humourless, uncompromising and detached, without picturesque idiosyncrasies—but with the power of explaining profound ideas in simple terms, of analysing a concrete situation. And combined with shrewdness, the greatest intellectual audacity."

Beginning his speech with "We shall now proceed to construct the Socialist order!", at the meeting, Lenin proposed a "Decree on Peace" calling for an end of the war, and a "Decree on Land" announcing that all property owned by large land owners and the aristocracy would be given to the peasants. Both decrees passed with little dissension. Next, the new government elected a Bolshevik majority to the Council of People's Commissars, with the Mensheviks joining the government a few weeks later. Lenin was soon elected Chairman of the Council, making him head of the government, though he had originally intended for the position to go to Trotsky, who declined because he worried his Jewish ethnicity would pose problems.

In recognition of his contribution, the now totally empowered Lenin appointed Stalin the Commissar of Nationalities, joking with him about his meteoric rise to power. As Commissar, Stalin was in charge of all the non-Russian people in the country, including Buriats, Byelorussians, Georgians, Tadzhiks, Ukrainians and Yakuts, nearly half the country's population. The spoiled little boy who'd been forced to speak Russian and had been teased about his appearance was now a bitter, angry man with nearly unlimited power. The combination would not make for a pretty outcome.

Initially, however, it looked like all would be well for these foreigners under Russian control. He concluded his famous Helsinki address of 1917 with these words of encouragement and promises of support:

> "Comrades! Information has reached us that your country is experiencing approximately the same crisis of power as Russia experienced on the eve of the October Revolution. Information has reached us that attempts are being made to frighten you too with the bogey of famine, sabotage, and so on. Permit me to tell you on the basis of the practical experience of the revolutionary movement in Russia that these dangers, even if real, are by no means insuperable! These dangers can be overcome if you act resolutely and without faltering. In the midst of war and economic disruption, in the midst of the revolutionary movement which is flaring up in the West and of the increasing victories of the workers' revolution in Russia, there are no dangers or difficulties that could withstand your onslaught. In such a situation only one power, socialist power, can maintain itself and conquer. In such a situation only one kind of tactics can be effective, the tactics of Danton—audacity, audacity and again audacity! And if you should need our help, you will have it—we shall extend you a fraternal hand. Of this you may rest assured."

Unfortunately, the non-Russian peoples who heard or read this speech remained unconvinced. They were not so much interested in Russian help as they were national determination. Therefore they proved to be a constant source of stress to the new Commissar, setting up their own governments, opposing Bolshevik policy, and overall acting with the self-determination they had been promised, as long as they determined to join the new Union of Soviet Socialist Republics.

Faced with this level of opposition to his and the other Bolsheviks' plans, Stalin took a different tact. Accusing the new independent governments of being under the control of "the bourgeoisie," he agreed with Lenin that a more centralized government was needed. As the Russian Civil War played out during the early 1920s, Stalin became more involved in military matters while Lenin continued to focus on politics.

Trotsky, meanwhile, had become chairman of the Petrograd Soviet in St. Petersburg (which had its name changed to Petrograd during World War I to sound less German). Trotsky regained his reputation as a fiery and charismatic speaker with great sway over the city's working class. At the same time, during and after his prison stint, he solidified his relations with the Bolsheviks and Lenin and finally joined the party, ending his status as a factionless coalition-builder and severing his earlier ties to the Mensheviks, who had been allied with Kerensky's governing coalition.

Ironically, Lenin did not think there would be be a need to create a political police force or external intelligence agency. In this, he was joined by Trotsky, who initially ordered the publication of the secret treaties signed by the tsarist government and asserted that "the rejection of secret diplomacy is the main condition for an honest, popular, genuinely democratic foreign policy" (Simbirdzev, 2017).

Lenin's pre-revolutionary idea of life in Bolshevik Russia was nothing more than a utopia. In *The State and Revolution*, written in the summer of 1917, he had argued that in the future there will be no place for the police, especially for the secret police. But things drastically changed when the Bolshevik leaders collided with reality. The fundamental element of the Soviet state was the communist myth that, as the vanguard of the proletariat, the Bolsheviks led a popular uprising that expressed the will not only of the Bolsheviks themselves, but of the entire Russian people. Actually, the October Revolution was nothing more than a coup d'état, committed by a revolutionary minority overthrowing the Provisional Government which itself had replaced the tsarist regime.

Neither Lenin nor his followers could accept this reality. Overthrowing the government that had lost the confidence of the people, the Bolsheviks still could not get or maintain the support of the vast majority. In the Constituent Assembly elections held immediately after the revolution, their main left opponents were the Socialist-Revolutionaries, who achieved the absolute majority of votes, while the Bolsheviks were able to win the support of less than a quarter of voters. Even in alliance with the Socialist-Revolutionaries, they remained in the minority, so they dissolved the Constituent Assembly, convened in January 1918.

Having seen how easily a multi-generational dynasty fell, Lenin was obviously concerned about keeping his own infant administration safe. Lenin did not expect that the new Bolshevik government (the Council of People's Commissars) would face such internal and external opposition, which is ultimately what led to his decition to create a "special machine" for solving this problem. Convinced of the uniqueness and exceptional correctness of Marxist doctrine, the Bolshevik leaders viewed any opposition, regardless of its social roots, as a threat of counter-revolution.

On December 19, it became known that a general strike of civil servants was coming. This news made the Council of People's Commissars and its chairman Lenin take more radical measures. Felix Dzerzhinsky received the instruction to create a special commission to resolve such kind of problems and combat counter-revolution. The next day, December 20, Lenin wrote to Dzerzhinsky, "The bourgeoisie intends to commit the most heinous crime..." Addressing the Council of People's Commissars on the same day, Dzerzhinsky required the creation of the commission to combat counter-revolution: "Do not think that I'm looking for forms of revolutionary justice. We do not need justice now, there is a war on the face to face, a war to the end, life or death (Archive of the Cheka, 2007).

Dzerzhinsky

Yakov Peters, Józef Unszlicht, Abram Belenky (standing), Dzerzhinsky, and Vyacheslav Menzhinsky at the presidium of the Cheka in 1921

Thus, the Council of People's Commissars approved the creation, under the leadership of Dzerzhinsky, of the All-Russian Extraordinary Commission for Combating Counter-Revolution and Sabotage, known subsequently as the Extraordinary Commission. Known colloquially as the Cheka (Extraordinary Commission), it soon became as feared by non-socialists as the Tsar's secret police had ever been. In addition to monitoring the movements of anyone opposing the government, the Cheka also enforced censorship laws against non-socialist newspapers.

The KGB has created a kind of cult of personality out of Dzerzhinskiy. In his address was uttered more words of praise than to all his followers taken together. Calling him the "knight of the revolution, Soviet historian V. Andrianov wrote, "There are many people who deserve this title, but despite this, every time we uttered these words, we primarily think of F. Dzerzhinsky ... Throughout his heroic life, he paved the way to immortality" (Sever, 2008).

Like most of the early leaders of the Cheka, Dzerzhinsky was not Russian by nationality. He was born in 1877 in the family of Polish intellectuals-landowners. In his early childhood, he believed that his vocation was to become a Catholic priest. However at school he became interested in Marxism and in 1895 joined the ranks of the Lithuanian Social-Democratic Party. In 1900 he became one of the founders of the Social Democratic Party of Poland and Lithuania (SDPiL), led by the famous German-Polish Marxist theorist Rosa Luxemburg. This party advocated not for the independence of Poland, but for proletarian internationalism and cooperation with Russian Marxists. He joined the Bolsheviks, first as a delegate to the SDPiL, and then he was elected to the Central Committee of the Bolshevik Party at the summer party conference of 1917. Later, Dzerzhinsky took an active part in the October Revolution.

Luxemburg

During his first year as head of the Cheka, Dzerzhinsky was working and living in his office in the Lubyanka in Moscow, and thanks to his Spartan lifestyle, he received the nickname "Iron Felix". The old Chekist (member of Cheka) Fyodor Timofeevich Fomin later reported with admiration that Dzerzhinsky refused to enjoy the privileges that the other Chekists did not have (Gordievskiy & Andru, 1992). Like Lenin, Dzerzhinsky was extremely efficient, and willing to sacrifice himself and others in the name of the ideals of the revolution. Viktor Chebrikov, chairman of the KGB from 1982-1988, stated, "Felix Edmundovich wanted to eradicate injustice and crimes on earth and dreamed of those times when wars and national enmity would disappear forever from our lives." (Ibid).

The cult of Dzerzhinsky was created immediately after his death in 1926. The portrait of Dzerzhinsky and his military uniform were placed in a glass coffin and exhibited in the conference room of the KGB officer club as an object of worship. During the celebration of the 20th anniversary of the Cheka in December 1937, Dzerzhinsky was called "an indefatigable

Bolshevik, an inflexible knight of the revolution, under whose leadership the Cheka repeatedly seized the mortal threat hanging over the young Soviet Republic." (Archive of the Cheka, 2007).

The cult of Stalin gradually supplanted the image of Dzerzhinsky. Soon after World War II, his portrait and posthumous mask were removed from the KGB officer's club, but the policy of de-Stalinization during the 1960s marked the beginning of the revival of the cult of Dzerzhinsky. The KGB tried in every possible way to dissociate itself from the bloody role that he played in the immediate wake of Lenin's death as Stalin took control, and a mythical portrait was created, depicting Dzerzhinsky (Saint Felix), as a "knight of the revolution" killing the dragon of the counter-revolution.

Dzerzhinsky's words that the Chekist should have a "hot heart, a cold head and clean hands" were transferred from one monument to another (Gordievskiy & Andru, 1992). In the late 1950s, opposite the central building of the KGB in Dzerzhinsky Square, a large statue of Dzerzhinsky was erected.

The main means approved by the Council of People's Commissars on December 20, 1917, which the Cheka had to use to fight the counter-revolution, were "seizure of property, resettlement, deprivation of cards, publication of lists of enemies of the people, etc". Nevertheless, the main weapon of the Cheka was terror. Lenin did not imagine the scale of the opposition he would have to face after the revolution, and he quickly came to the conclusion that "a special system of organized violence" must be created to implement the dictatorship of the proletariat. Lenin brutally criticized the "prejudices on the death penalty." (Ibid)

All the while, Lenin believed that the masses had healthier instincts. In December 1917, Lenin suggested that the masses should execute their own court ("street court") over "speculators". He strongly encouraged all actions, including terror, directed against "class enemies". One of his closest associates, Martin Yanovich Latsis, wrote in the newspaper *Krasny Terror*, "We do not wage war against individual people, we are destroying the bourgeoisie as a class. (Ibid)

In January 1918, despite objections from Lenin and Dzerzhinsky, the representatives of the Left Socialist-Revolutionaries in the Council of People's Commissars insisted on their party representation in the Cheka. One of the four left-wing Socialist-Revolutionaries appointed by members of the Cheka board, Vyacheslav Alekseevich Alexandrovich, became the deputy of Dzerzhinsky. In March 1918, after signing peace with Germany in Brest-Litovsk, as a sign of protest, the Left Socialist-Revolutionaries withdrew from the Council of People's Commissars. The Bolshevik Party changed its name to the Communist Party. Since then, the Council of People's Commissars was composed exclusively of Communists, and the Bolshevik government moved the capital from Petrograd to Moscow, ironically in part because its treaty with Germany ending the war placed potential enemy forces too close to Petrograd for comfort.

Despite the fact that the Left Socialist Revolutionaries left the government, they were still a part of the Cheka, and Dzerzhinsky fully trusted his deputy, Aleksandrovich. After moving to Moscow, he handed over to him the full power of solving daily administrative issues, and he concentrated on his operational work.

One of the first victims of the Chekist terror in Moscow was the famous circus clown Bim-Bom, who often laughed at the Communists. As it would be with the KGB, the Cheka did not understand such humor and considered it as an ideological provocation. When the Chekists with stony faces approached Bim-Bom, viewers thought that this was only part of the overall performance, but their laughter soon gave way to a panic when they heard the shots. The Chekists opened fire on Bim-Bohm, who was trying to escape.

In addition to terror, in the fight against counter-revolution, the Cheka often used the agents. Although Dzerzhinsky opposed the royal (tsarist) methods of using agent provocateurs, he very quickly became a real expert in this field. According to KGB sources, the first significant success of the Cheka using its agents was an operation against an organization that was in Petrograd known as the "Union to Combat the Bolsheviks".

A Chekist known as Golubev, posing as a former officer of the tsarist army, was able to quickly penetrate into the Union, expose many of its members, and reveal the places of their secret encounters. During January and February, the entire "Union", numbering about 4,000 people, was exposed by the Chekists and completely neutralized with the help of the Red Guards. The Bolsheviks believed that the entire Western capitalist world was revolting against them with all its might, and the Chekists believed they would play the decisive role in protecting the young Soviet state in its struggle against the gigantic conspiracies of the Western capital system and its secret services.

In spite of the Cheka's best efforts, those who opposed Lenin and the Bolsheviks were still out there, and they were gunning for Lenin, literally. In January 1918, gunmen shot at Lenin and Fritz Platten as they sat in an automobile after Lenin had given a speech, which Lenin survived after Platten pushed him down and shielded him. But the most famous assassination attempt would come in August 1918, when a supporter of the Socialist Revolutionary Party, Fanya Kaplan, approached Lenin as he sat in an automobile. After calling to him to get his attention, she fired at him three times, hitting him once in the arm and once in the jaw and neck. Though the wounds rendered him unconscious, Lenin survived the shooting, and fearful of people at the hospital who might try to finish the job, he returned to the Kremilin and ordered physicians to come there to treat him where he felt safe. Ultimately, doctors refused to perform surgery given the precarious position of the bullet in his neck. Pravda used the attempt for propaganda purposes, reporting, "Lenin, shot through twice, with pierced lungs spilling blood, refuses help and goes on his own. The next morning, still threatened with death, he reads papers, listens, learns, and observes to see that the engine of the locomotive that carries us towards global revolution has not stopped working..."

Fanya Kaplan

Despite that, Soviet officials began to downplay the attack, and many across Russia never learned of it. Though he survived the attack, the bullets were left in place and continued to erode his health. However, Lenin kept working and appearing in public, determined to keep the public ignorant of how weak his condition was becoming. This was important because Lenin was increasingly viewed as the embodiment of the new regime, and it was feared that his death could cause everything to crumble. One former Tsarist wrote as much, reporting after the attempt, "As it happens, the attempt to kill Lenin has made him much more popular than he was. One hears a great many people, who are far from having any sympathy with the Bolsheviks, saying that it would be an absolute disaster if Lenin had succumbed to his wounds, as it was first thought he would. And they are quite right, for, in the midst of all this chaos and confusion, he is the backbone of the new body politic, the main support on which everything rests.."

The Bolsheviks may have downplayed the assassination attempt publicly, but they were privately plotting retaliation on a massive scale. Two weeks before Kaplan's attempt on Lenin's life, the Petrograd Cheka chief Moisei Uritsky had been assassinated, and now Stalin suggested to Lenin that they should engage in "open and systematic mass terror…[against] those responsible." Thus, the Cheka, under the instruction of Stalin, launched what later came to be known as the "Red Terror" in response to the assassination attempt. In the weeks that followed, more than 800 people were executed, including the entire Romanov family. This however, was just the beginning. As the Bolsheviks, known popularly as the Red Russians fought an ongoing war against those who opposed socialism (the White Russians), more than 18,000 people were executed on charges related to opposing Lenin and his rule. While historians have often debated the extent of Lenin's personal involvement in the executions, Trotsky himself later asserted that it was Lenin who authorized the execution of the Russian Royal Family.

Though he is often remembered as a vocal opponent of Stalin's terror (and ultimately a victim of it), Trotsky was fully in support of the Cheka's methods and even took time to write and publish a full-throated defense of them in the book *Terrorism and Communism* (1920). He also defended the policies of "War Communism," including large-scale confiscation of produce, livestock, and grains in order to fuel the war effort, practices that placed a devastating burden on the rural poor in particular. Trotsky summed up his defense of all of these measures in *Terrorism and Communism*: "The more perfect the revolution, the greater are the masses it draws in; and the longer it is prolonged, the greater is the destruction it achieves in the apparatus of production, and the more terrible inroads does it make upon public resources. From this there follows merely the conclusion which did not require proof – that a civil war is harmful to economic life. But to lay this at the door of the Soviet economic system is like accusing a new-born human being of the birth-pangs of the mother who brought him into the world."

Victims of the Red Terror

Imperial Germany was the only power that established official diplomatic relations with the Bolshevik regime and exchanged ambassadors after the signing of the peace the treaty in Brest-Litovsk. On April 23, 1918 in Moscow, the German Embassy was opened, headed by Graph Wilhelm Mirbach.

The task of penetrating the German embassy was entrusted to the counter-intelligence department, created in May 1918 in the framework of combating counter-revolution. In 1921-1922 the counterintelligence department (abbreviated as KRO) was expanded and become the predecessor of the Second Main Directorate of the KGB. At the head of this department was the twenty-year-old left-wing Socialist-Revolutionary Yakov Blumkin, perhaps the youngest head of the department in the history of the KGB. Blumkin successfully carried out the operation to penetrate the German embassy, having come into contact with Count Robert Mirbach, an

Austrian relative of the German ambassador, who was captured during the war. In June, Blumkin received from him a written commitment to supply the Cheka with secret information about Germany and the activities of the German embassy.

However, Dzerzhinsky acted unreasonably, entrusting this operation to Blumkin, since the Left Socialist-Revolutionaries continued to actively oppose the Brest-Litovsk Peace Agreement. On July 4, the Central Committee of the Left SRs approved the plan of the assassination of the German ambassador. The Left SRs believed that by killing him they would force the Bolsheviks to stop the "pacification" of the Germans and resume military operations on the Eastern Front, which, in their opinion, would contribute to the cause of the development of the world revolution.

The attempt was directed to Blumkin and his collaborator, photographer, left-wing Socialist-Revolutionary, Nikolai Andreev. On the morning of July 6, Blumkin prepared a document on the letterhead of the Cheka, with the forged signature of Dzerzhinsky and the secretary of the Cheka, instructing him and Andreev to negotiate with the German ambassador.

Dzerzhinsky's assistant, the Left Socialist-Revolutionary Aleksandrovich, who was involved in this conspiracy by Bliumkin, put an official seal of the Cheka on this document. In the afternoon of the same day Blyumkin and Andreev came to the German embassy and agreed to meet with the ambassador under the pretext of having to discuss the matter connected with his relative Count Robert Mirbach. Later Blumkin claimed that he killed the ambassador from his revolver, however, according to the embassy's staff, all three shots done by Blumkin failed to achieve the goal, and Count Wilhelm Mirbach was killed by Andreev. (Sever, 2008).

Thus, instead of defending a new communist state, in July 1918 the Cheka almost did not play the role of an instrument for its destruction. In a telegram to Stalin, Lenin wrote that the assassination of Mirbach put Russia on "the verge of a resumption of war with Germany" (Archive of the Cheka, 2007). The assassination was followed by the uprising of the Left Socialist-Revolutionaries, as a result of which the building of the Cheka in the Lubyanka was seized, and Dzerzhinsky was arrested. But the Left SRs had no clear plan of action, and their rebellion was suppressed within 24 hours by Communists Latvian troops.

On July 8, at his own request, Dzerzhinsky resigned from his post as head of the Cheka. A commission was set up to investigate the circumstances of the uprising, and the Cheka was cleaned of the Left SRs. August 22 Dzerzhinsky was again appointed to the post of chairman of the Cheka. By this time, the Cheka consisted exclusively of Communists. The restraining influence of the Left Socialist-Revolutionaries had lost its force, and the policy of terror against political enemies had been developed.

Meanwhile, the forces of the so-called White Army, made up of anti-Bolshevik Russians of all stripes and their allies from nearly all the major European nations, combined to place the new revolutionary regime in a state of siege. In response, the Bolsheviks introduced a number of policies that would set the stage for the state terrorism and suppression of later years.

White Army propaganda poster depicting Trotsky as Satan

Unfortunately, bullets weren't all that was killing the Russian common people. While the Whites and Reds engaged in a civil war that would last for nearly 7 years, ordinary Russians were starving due to war time communism measures that allowed the Soviet government to confiscate food for soldiers from peasant farms with little or no payment. When the farmers retaliated by growing fewer crops, the Cheka responded by executing or imprisoning the offending peasants. However, even the Cheka could not cause plants to grow, and during the Famine of 1921, more than 5 million Russians starved to death in and near their own homes.

This tragedy, along with the civil unrest it provoked, led Lenin to institute the New Economic Policy to rejuvenate the both agriculture and industry.

As this all suggests, the cruelty of the Cheka can be compared with Stalin's NKVD (People's Commissariat of Internal Affairs of the USSR), although the scale of the massacres was much less at this time. While Dzerzhinsky and his assistants resorted to the Red Terror only as an objectively necessary means of class struggle, some of the ordinary members of the Cheka, especially in the provinces, enjoyed the power of cruelty without going into high ideological discourse. Yakov Khristoforovich Peter, one of Dzerzhinsky's first and most prominent assistants, later recognized the existence of "many dishonest elements" in the Cheka (Archive of the Cheka, 2007).

Reorganizing the Cheka

The Cheka's badge in the early 1920s

By the beginning of the 1920s, the White Guard forces no longer posed a serious threat to the Bolshevik regime, although they were not completely destroyed. The decree signed by Lenin and

Dzerzhinsky abolished the death penalty for "enemies of Soviet power," but three weeks later Lenin changed his mind. At a meeting of representatives of the local Cheka, he said that the death penalty was only "a necessary measure", which, most likely, would also be needed for further struggle against "counter-revolutionary movements." (Archive of the Cheka, 2007). In the official history of the KGB, it says, "Thanks to the determined struggle of the Cheka authorities, the plans of the White Poles were failed, aimed at undermining the Red Army's fighting efficiency through espionage, sabotage and banditry." (Ibid)

Between 1917 and 1921, more than 250,000 people became victims of the Cheka, but by 1921, when the victory of the Bolsheviks in the Civil War was no longer in doubt, many members of the party believed that the Cheka's time had passed. Naturally, the Chekists opposed the thought of disbanding, and although the growth of the Cheka was temporarily stopped, and its rights were limited, it still managed to survive, albeit in a slightly modified form. The 9th All-Russian Congress of Soviets noted on December 28, 1921 that "the strengthening of Soviet power in the country and abroad has made it possible to reduce the functions of the Cheka and its bodies." (Ibid).

Soviet Russia began to take a number of steps to implement a large-scale program of secret activities outside the country even before systematic collection of information on the channels of foreign intelligence was established. While the Cheka was protecting the Bolshevik regime from real and imaginary enemies within the country, the activities of Soviet agents abroad were primarily aimed at spreading the revolution. At the same time, most foreign secret operations were organized not by the Cheka, but by the Comintern, the Communist International, which was under the control of the Bolsheviks. The Executive Committee of the Comintern (IKKI) called itself the "General Staff of the World Revolution." (Collins, 1998).

The collection of intelligence information abroad had become increasingly important. Despite the considerable successes of Soviet espionage activity in the 1920s, the main object of the Cheka's activity from the first day of its foundation was "counterrevolution", and not capitalist governments. Until the end of the Civil War, the main threat of counterrevolution came from within Russia itself, but with the evacuation of the last White Guard armies in November 1920, the counter-revolutionary centers moved abroad. On December 1, 1920, Lenin instructed Dzerzhinsky to develop a plan for the neutralization of these centers. Four days later, Dzerzhinsky presented a multi-purpose plan of action. He offered to take more hostages from family members of eminent Russian emigres, create special detachments to attack its leaders, and expand operations with the use of agent-provocateurs.

Thus, on December 20, 1920, the third anniversary of the Cheka's establishment, Dzerzhinsky decided to create the Foreign Department (better known as INO). On February 8, 1922, the Cheka was transformed into the State Political Administration (GPU), which became part of the People's Commissariat of Internal Affairs (NKVD). Dzerzhinsky, who headed the Commissariat of Internal Affairs and the Cheka since March 1919, became the head of the GPU.

Officially, the rights of the GPU were significantly reduced in comparison with what the Cheka had. The field of activity of the GPU was narrowed to the organization and conduct of subversive operations, while all issues related to criminal offenses were now settled by courts and revolutionary tribunals. The GPU was given the right only to conduct an investigation, meaning it was no longer able to pass sentence without trial or exile people to concentration camps administratively.

Ultimately, however, the GPU was gradually able to regain most of the rights that the Cheka had, and this was done with the blessing of Lenin. After the creation of the USSR in 1923, the GPU was given the status of a union body (United State Political Administration, abbreviated OGPU). Unlike the Cheka, conceived as a temporarily necessary means to protect the revolution in its infancy, the GPU, OGPU and their followers occupied one of the central places in the Soviet state system.

Stalin and Spying

In 1926, Dzerzhinsky died of a heart attack, and Vyacheslav Rudolfovich Menzhinsky was appointed in place of Dzerzhinsky. At first glance, both Dzerzhinsky and Menzhinsky had much in common, most notably as old Bolsheviks and descendants of wealthy Polish families. Menzhinsky became a member of the Cheka board shortly after its foundation and was appointed as the first deputy of Dzerzhinsky when he became chairman of the OGPU. He may also have been the most educated among the leaders of the KGB - Menzhinsky was fluent in 12 languages when he was hired by the Cheka, and he subsequently learned Chinese, Japanese, Persian and Turkish. He was also interested in physics, chemistry, astronomy, and mathematics.

Menzhinsky

Menzhinsky was not a follower of Stalin's, which would naturally put him in a precarious position moving forward. During the Civil War, he met Trotsky at the front and warned that Stalin was leading a "very complicated game" against him. However, he never seriously opposed the growing power of Stalin.

Before his new appointment, Menzhinsky was suffering from asthma, so he often met visitors while lying on the couch in his office in Lubyanka. In April 1929, Menzhinsky suffered a heart attack that sidelined him for two years. In 1931, he returned to perform his duties, but his health did not allow him to work hard.

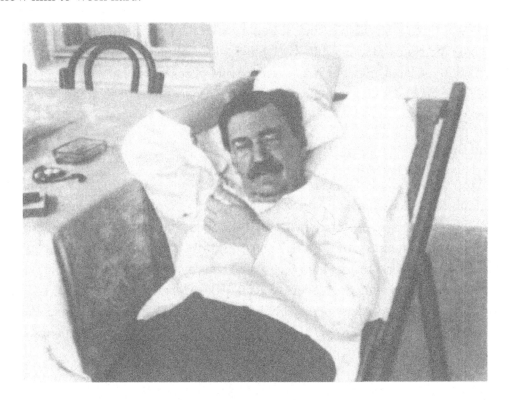

Due to Menzhinsky's poor health and his sluggish leadership, the power in the OGPU gradually shifted to his more aggressive deputy, Henry Grigorevich Yagoda. According to Aghabekov, if Menzhinsky had no equal in breadth of education, Yagoda had no equal in cruelty, lack of culture, and rudeness (Ibid). However, these traits had not yet manifested themselves so clearly when Dzerzhinsky appointed him as his second deputy in 1923. Perhaps Dzerzhinsky believed that he was simply an executive and energetic bureaucrat, full of ambition, but if so, Yagoda became a classic example of a bureaucrat spoiled by excessive power.

Yagoda

Stalin never completely trusted Yagoda and bided his time waiting for a convenient moment to change the head of the OGPU. Stalin was able to negotiate with Yagoda, who was more a careerist than an ideologist and was ready to follow Stalin merely to climb the social ladder. At the same time, he was not ready to support Stalin unconditionally.

During its first year under the leadership of Menzhinsky and Yagoda, the OGPU successfully completed an operation called "Trust," but this success was overshadowed by a number of scandalous exposures and failures of Soviet foreign intelligence. In the spring of 1927, a sensational exposure of Soviet agents took place in 8 different countries. That March, an espionage organization was uncovered in Poland, led by a former White Army general who later became an agent of the OGPU named Daniel Vetrenko. Around the same time, the leading specialist of the Soviet-Turkish corporation in Istanbul was accused of organizing espionage on the Turkish-Iraqi border. Shortly after, the Swiss police announced the arrest of two Soviet spies, and in April, during a search conducted at the Soviet consulate in Beijing, a huge number of documents on Soviet espionage activities were found. The French "Surte" also arrested 8 members of the Soviet espionage network headed by Jean Creme, a member of the Politburo of the French Communist Party. In May, officers of the Austrian Ministry of Foreign Affairs were detained, and they supplied the OGPU agents with secret information. And as a result of a raid and search conducted by British special services in London on the premises of the All-Russian Cooperative Society ("Arcos") and the Soviet trade delegation, William Joneson-Hicks, the Minister of Internal Affairs of the Great Britain, claimed that "one of the biggest and most nefarious espionage organizations was disclosed." (Gordievskiy & Andru, 1992).

The police raids in Beijing and London, followed by the publication of some intelligence information, dealt a strong blow to the Soviet foreign spy network. The documents published in China contained a lot of scandalous details about the activities of the Soviet secret agencies (mainly military intelligence), including instructions received from Moscow that "no measures, including robbery and massacres, should be avoided" in promoting conflict between the Chinese people and Western countries (Ibid). They also contained lists of agents' names, instructions to Chinese communists to assist in conducting intelligence operations, and detailed descriptions of weapons secretly imported into China.

The exposures of Soviet spies had another serious consequence, as relations between the Soviet Union and Great Britain were formally broken. The USSR used to consider Great Britain as the world's leading power, but the exposure of activities of the Soviet military intelligence in 1927 was the last straw. On May 26, 1927, Austen Chamberlain informed the Soviet attorney Arkady Rozengolts that the British government was breaking diplomatic relations with the Soviet Union, since it conducted "anti-British, espionage activities and propaganda." (Ibid).

The exposure of Soviet intelligence in the spring of 1927 had a significant impact on Stalin, who viewed it all as evidence of a deep imperialist conspiracy. He claimed, "There is no doubt that the main question of our time is the question of the threat of an imperialist war. This is not some kind of unreal, immaterial 'danger' of a new war. This is a very real, material threat of war in general and war against the Soviet Union in particular." According to Stalin, the first organizer of the "United Imperialist Front" against the Soviet Union was its main enemy, "the British bourgeoisie and its general headquarters—the Conservative Party." In response, the OGPU, as the "shield and sword of the revolution," would be called upon to disclose and expose the inevitable imperialist conspiracies and nip them in the bud.

For the first time, Stalin used the OGPU to strengthen his power within the Communist Party. Like the Cheka, the OGPU aimed to combat the counter-revolution, but now, the definition of the counter-revolution had changed. Under Lenin, the counter-revolution meant an opposition to the Communist Party, whereas under Stalin, it simply meant opposition to Stalin himself. Since many Communists were opposed to Stalin, the OGPU used the same methods of penetration and provocation inside the party that had previously been used against enemies of the party.

The first victims were members of the "Left Opposition," headed by Trotsky and Zinoviev. In November 1927, Trotsky, Zinoviev, and almost 100 of their followers were expelled from the party. Zinoviev agreed to repent and renounce "Trotskyism," after which he was reinstated in the ranks of the party. Trotsky refused to do so, and in January 1928, he was exiled by the OGPU to a remote region of Kazakhstan along the border with China.

Zinoviev

Having finished with the "Left Opposition," Stalin aimed to realize his radical policy of the Socialist reorganization of the Soviet economy. Addressing the Central Committee in November 1928, Stalin insisted that the survival of Socialism in a country depended on the ability of the Soviet economy to overtake the West.

Meanwhile, a new threat of external aggression spurred the hunt of internal saboteurs who had entered into an alliance with foreigners, especially with the French "imperialists." On September 22, 1930, it was announced in the press that the OGPU had discovered a "counter-revolutionary society" consisting of 48 professors, agronomists, and heads of food enterprises, led by Professor Alexander Ryazantsev. All of them were accused of disrupting food supplies and were shot.

Stalin and many members of the OGPU continued to believe the counter-revolutionary conspiracies of traitors and foreign enemies were part of a long-term plan for sabotaging the Soviet economy. In March 1933, six English electrical engineers of the Metropolitan Vickers Company who had worked on the construction of one of Russia's industrial facilities were charged with sabotage and espionage and arrested as a result. In response, the British government announced a trade embargo, which was canceled in July 1933 after the British engineers were released.

In July 1934, the OGPU was renamed the GUGB (Main Directorate of State Security) and transferred to the newly opened NKVD (People's Commissariat of Internal Affairs) headed by Yagoda. Thus, the political police, the regular police, the criminal investigation service, the border troops, the internal troops, and the entire criminal system all became subordinate to one body in October 1934, and the NKVD became synonymous with the political police, although it was formally a part of the latter. This powerful machine was personally and directly subordinate to Stalin, who had a direct line of communication with the NKVD through his personal secretariat, headed by Alexander Poskrebyshev.

In 1936, Nikolai Ezhov replaced Yagoda as chairman of the NKVD and headed the "Great Terror." The murder of Sergey Kirov, Stalin's main potential opponent, led to an even greater strengthening of the NKVD's power. On December 1, 1934, Kirov was shot from behind as he left his office in the central building of the party organization in Leningrad. Leonid Nikolaev, his assassin, considered himself a follower of the "populists" who had committed the assassination of Tsar Alexander II and had obvious mental problems.

Kirov

Shortly before the assassination, Nikolaev was twice detained by Kirov's guards and released both times on orders from the Leningrad NKVD, despite the fact that a loaded revolver had been found in his briefcase. None of the KGB officers had any doubt that Stalin personally gave the order to kill Kirov, and many believe Stalin decided not to give this case to Yagoda, whom he did not fully trust. Instead, he acted through the head of the Leningrad NKVD, Philip Medved, and his deputy, I. Zaporozhets (Gordievskiy and Andru, 1992).

After Kirov's assassination, a directive came into force the same evening requiring the immediate punishment of all those suspected of terrorism, including the death penalty. According to Nikita Khrushchev, this directive came out "without the approval of the Politburo," meaning it was Stalin's personal initiative. Thus, the NKVD gained power over the life and death of Soviet citizens. For the next 20 years, the NKVD determined who was a "terrorist" and who was not.

The first victims of the NKVD, those accused of Kirov's death, were the so-called White Guard conspirators who had penetrated Russia through the border with Poland, Finland, and Latvia. 104 fictional conspirators were captured and shot.

In 1935, Stalin aimed to organize massive attacks on the existing and potential opposition to his regime. The purge of the party in 1933 and 1934 was mainly aimed at eradicating "corruption," and in 1935, the purge intensified and became more politicized. At Stalin's behest in the summer of 1936, the Central Committee approved a secret resolution giving the NKVD the extraordinary power to destroy all "enemies of the people."

Nikolai Ivanovich Yezhov who had come to replace Yagoda, was the first Russian to become the head of the KGB. As secretary of the Central Committee and head of the Control Commission, Yezhov had supervised the activities of the NKVD on behalf of Stalin. He also created a security service parallel to the NKVD inside the party apparatus.

During Yezhov's time, all restrictions preventing the elimination of Stalin's imaginary enemies were removed. On June 11, it was announced that Marshal Tukhachevsky, a hero of the Russian Civil War and a leading Soviet military strategist, was arrested, along with seven other generals, on charges of treason. They were apparently shot the next day, and Marshal Voroshilov reported that the traitors had "confessed to their crimes, sabotage and espionage."(Gordievskiy and Andru, 1992). As it was later announced, they'd conspired with Trotsky and Nazi Germany.

Yezhov

The most dangerous "enemies of the people" were the employees of three organizations called upon to defend the Soviet state, the party, the Red Army, and the NKVD. 110 of the 139 members of the Central Committee elected at the party Congress in 1934 were shot or sentenced to imprisonment. Perhaps not surprisingly, only 59 of 1,966 delegates took part in the work of the next Congress in 1939. 75 of the 80 members of the Revolutionary Military Council were shot, and more than half of the officers of the Red Army, probably more than 35,000 people, were shot or imprisoned. The top leadership of the NKVD itself was changed twice (ibid).

Under Yezhov, all 18 state security commissioners of the first and second ranks who had served under Yagoda were shot, with the exception of Slutsky, who was poisoned. Of the 122 top officers serving from 1937-1938, only 21 officers managed to maintain their position after Yezhov himself fell victim to Stalin's purges and was executed in 1940. During his leadership, anything that remained of the first Cheka leaders' idealism had been destroyed. Yezhov was convinced their cruelty was necessary for building a new society and fighting counter-revolution.

Victims of the NKVD were both Russian and foreign Communists. Most of the representatives of the Comintern and foreign communist parties in Moscow were exposed as "enemy agents" or "foreign spies" and shot. The most vulnerable were members of illegal Communist parties and their families, as they could not count on the support of the countries from which they had come. Most of them had been sentenced to prisons abroad and were therefore accused of being recruited by capitalist special services.

Of all the illegal parties, the most fictitious of spies were among the leadership of the Polish and Yugoslav Communist Parties. Polish Communists caused the greatest suspicion, as there were many Jews among their leaders who took Trotsky's side after Lenin's death, and they were shot. Stalin also did not trust the Yugoslav Communist Party, headed by S. Markovich, who, in 1925, opposed the Stalinist approach to the solution of the national question. Paradoxically, Stalin used to trust Marshal Tito, the Communist leader in Yugoslavia.

Tito

The last large-scale exposure of a fictional international counter-revolutionary conspiracy against Stalin's Russia came in February 1938 with the trial of 21 members of the "bloc of Rightists and Trotskyists." The main defendants were Bukharin, Rykov, and Yagoda, who stood accused of an expanded version of the usual set of "Trotskyist crimes," including espionage, sabotage, terrorism, preparation for foreign invasion, the dismemberment of the USSR, the overthrow of Soviet power, and the restoration of capitalism. Previously, Trotskyists had only conspired with the German and Japanese secret services, but now they were accused of cooperating with British and Polish intelligence services as well.

On the basis of Leninist principles, the imperialists were always trying to destroy the only workers-peasants' state in the world, so if they'd planned to destroy it, it was only natural to assume their intelligence services would actively work against the Soviet Union. In Stalin's opinion, it would be "absurd and stupid" to believe external enemies of the USSR would not attack him at their first opportunity, and those who did not share Stalin's conspiracy theories were immediately considered "enemies of the people."

With the government and army thoroughly cleansed of opposition, Stalin attacked the Communist Secret Police. In July 1938, Lavrenty Beria, the head of the Transcaucasian NKVD, was appointed as the First Deputy under Yezhov, and after that, the real power gradually passed into the hands of Beria. Beria was charged with ferreting out what he called "fascist elements" that he claimed had infiltrated the police force. In reality, it was Beria's job to round up those who knew the details behind the recent killing spree and to see to it that they were silenced. In doing this, he had every leader of the police force executed.

Beria

Under Beria, repression was selective, but the hunt for Trotsky continued in full force during this time. Since being exiled, Trotsky had constantly been on the move, including spending four years in Turkey, followed by periods living in France, Norway, and finally Mexico, where he remained until his death in 1940. He continued to write at a furious pace throughout this period, composing his own history of the 1917 Revolution and a detailed analysis of what he regarded as the perversion of socialism by Stalin's bureaucracy, which he expounded on in detail in his book *The Revolution Betrayed* (1936). At the same time, he organized an international movement of communists opposed to what was now called "Stalinism", a project that culminated in the creation of the Fourth International as an alternative to the Third International, the global communist organization now controlled by the Soviet state.

Trotsky reading the *Militant* in exile

Trotsky was a vocal and tireless critic of Stalin's grotesque "show trials," the humiliating convictions of Bolshevik leaders for alleged counter-revolutionary subversion. In the foreword of *The Stalin School of Falsification*, Trotsky wrote, "THE MOSCOW TRIALS, which so shocked the world, signify the death agony of Stalinism. A political regime constrained to use such methods is doomed. Depending upon external and internal circumstances, this agony may endure for a longer or shorter period of time. But no power in the world can any longer save Stalin and his system. The Soviet regime will either rid itself of the bureaucratic shell or be sucked into the abyss."

It was through this criticism that Trotsky gained his reputation as an advocate of a humane and democratic socialism. Trotsky's earlier writings about the use of Red Terror make that reputation problematic at best and disingenuous and flatly wrong at worst, but Trotskyist organizations did ultimately become an incubator of dissenting, non-doctrinaire leftist movements.

Even though he was exiled half a world away, Stalin feared his rival's growing international status, and he was never squeamish about the need for extreme methods to silence a potential enemy. Trotsky himself seemed prepared for the possibility. In May 1940, a cadre of Spanish and Mexican communists loyal to Stalin, including the important Mexican painter David Alfaro Siqueiros, assaulted Trotsky's home in an attempted hit. Trotsky survived, but he knew this would not be the last attempt against him.

Trotsky with supporters in 1940

Trotsky wouldn't be so lucky the second time around. On August 20, 1940, a Stalinist agent of Spanish origin named Ramón Mercader entered Trotsky's home and plunged an ice pick into his skull. Mercader later testified at his trial, "I laid my raincoat on the table in such a way as to be able to remove the ice axe which was in the pocket. I decided not to miss the wonderful opportunity that presented itself. The moment Trotsky began reading the article, he gave me my chance; I took out the ice axe from the raincoat, gripped it in my hand and, with my eyes closed, dealt him a terrible blow on the head."

Incredibly, the badly injured Trotsky was able to fight off his attacker with the help of his bodyguards, but he died the following day. His last words were allegedly, "I will not survive this attack. Stalin has finally accomplished the task he attempted unsuccessfully before."

The Birth of East Germany

As the Soviets turned the tide against the Nazi invasion of Russia, they were able to begin advancing west toward Germany themselves, but the Soviet armies would pay dearly for the advances they made on Germany after Hitler's invasion of Russia ended in failure: "According to the Soviet Union's estimates, the Red Army's losses in the war totaled more than 11 million troops, over 100,000 aircraft, more than 300,000 artillery pieces, and 100,000 tanks and self-propelled guns".[1] Such losses, coupled with the extreme suffering that the Soviet soldiers had experienced in the years before the attack on Berlin, ensured that the thirst for revenge would be

---

[1] Evans, Richard. *The Third Reich at War.* 707.

high upon arrival. Moreover, as the Soviet armies moved through Eastern Europe, they were the first to discover concentration camps and death camps, furthering their anger. The comparison of Germany's standard of living with their own was another cause of outrage, all of which encouraged the men to show no mercy: "We will take revenge…revenge for all our sufferings…It's obvious from everything we see that Hitler robbed the whole of Europe to please his Fritzies…Their shops are piled high with goods from all the shops and factories of Europe. We hate Germany and the Germans deeply. You can often see civilians lying dead in the street…But the Germans deserve the atrocities that they unleashed."[2]

Meanwhile, Germany's losses were mounting, and the Soviet armies were on the rebound, with an advantage of almost 5:1 over Germany in manpower, as well as superiority in tanks, aircraft, and artillery. Even with these major advantages, however, the race to Berlin would inflict a heavier toll on Soviet armies than they had yet seen, and with Berlin itself heavily defended by 30 mile deep defenses in multiple directions, the Soviets would eventually suffer over 100,000 lives just taking the city, along with 350,000 other casualties.

In the months leading up to the Battle of Berlin, there was a strange division amongst the German people regarding their fate. While Hitler called for the remainder of Berlin's population to take up arms and the most loyal responded to the call, many in Berlin were resigned to a seemingly inevitable defeat. In his study of Berlin in 1945, historian Antony Beevor described a city in which a grim humor had come to replace once hopeful and proud demeanors. Though humor was certainly an attempt at levity in the face of serious concerns, Germans nevertheless joked about the soon-to-arrive Russians, referring to LSR (Luftschutzraum air-raid shelters) as actually standing for "Lernt scnhell Russich" ("Learn Russian quickly").[3] In the air raid shelters, Berliners regularly found themselves in crowded conditions, waiting out the bombing raids that were taking place on a regular basis in 1944. In a city of 3 million, Beevor explained how a tightly-packed and unsanitary atmosphere became an expected part of life in Berlin. By the year's end, much of the city's beauty and a great deal of its functionality had been destroyed.

---

[2] Ibid., 708.
[3] Beevor, Antony. *The Fall of Berlin 1945*. New York: Penguin Books, 2003.

A picture of damage done to Berlin during a 1944 air raid

Things weren't going any better for Germany to the west either. After the successful amphibious invasion on D-Day in June 1944, the Allies began racing east toward Germany and liberating France along the way. The Allies had landed along a 50 mile stretch of French coast, and despite suffering 8,000 casualties on D-Day, over 100,000 still began the march across the western portion of the continent. By the end of August 1944, the German army in France was shattered, with 200,000 killed or wounded and a further 200,000 captured. However, Hitler reacted to the news of invasion with glee, figuring it would give the Germans a chance to destroy the Allied armies that had water to their backs. As he put it, "The news couldn't be better. We have them where we can destroy them."

While that sounds delusional in retrospect, it was Hitler's belief that by splitting the Allied march across Europe in their drive toward Germany, he could cause the collapse of the enemy armies and cut off their supply lines. Part of Hitler's confidence came as a result of underestimating American resolve, but with the Soviets racing toward Berlin from the east, this final offensive would truly be the last gasp of the German war machine, and the month long campaign was fought over a large area of the Ardennes Forest, through France, Belgium and parts of Luxembourg. From an Allied point of view, the operations were commonly referred to as the Ardennes Offensive, while the German code phrase for the operation was Unternehmen Wacht am Rhein ("Operation Watch on the Rhine"), with the initial breakout going under the name of "Operation Mist." Today, it is best known as the Battle of the Bulge.

Regardless of the term for it, and despite how desperate the Germans were, the Battle of the Bulge was a massive attack against primarily American forces that inflicted an estimated 100,000 American casualties, the heaviest American loss in any battle of the war. However, while the German forces did succeed in bending and at some points even breaking through Allied lines (thus causing the "bulge" reflected in the moniker), the Germans ultimately failed. As Winston Churchill himself said of the battle, "This is undoubtedly the greatest American battle of the war, and will, I believe be regarded as an ever famous American victory."

The end of the Battle of the Bulge led to the historic Yalta Conference between Roosevelt, Churchill, and Stalin from January 30-February 3. It was not lost on anyone present that the Allies were pushing the Nazis back on both fronts and the war in Europe was ending. The Big Three held the conference with the intention of redrawing the post-war map, but within a few years, the Cold War divided the continent anyway. As a result, Yalta became a subject of intense controversy, and to some extent, it has remained controversial. Among the agreements, the Conference called for Germany's unconditional surrender, the split of Berlin, and German demilitarization and reparations. Stalin, Churchill and Roosevelt also discussed the status of Poland, and Russian involvement in the United Nations.

The three leaders at Yalta

By this time, Stalin had thoroughly established Soviet authority in most of Eastern Europe and made it clear that he had no intention of giving up lands his soldiers had fought and died for. The best he would offer Churchill and Roosevelt was the promise that he would allow free elections to be held, but at the same time, he made clear that the only acceptable outcome to any Polish election would be one that supported communism. One Allied negotiator would later describe Stalin's very formidable negotiating skills: "Marshal Stalin as a negotiator was the toughest proposition of all. Indeed, after something like thirty years' experience of international conferences of one kind and another, if I had to pick a team for going into a conference room, Stalin would be my first choice. Of course the man was ruthless and of course he knew his purpose. He never wasted a word. He never stormed, he was seldom even irritated."

The final question was over what to do with a conquered Germany. The British, Americans and Russians all wanted Berlin, and they knew that whoever held the most of it when the truce was signed would end up controlling the city. Thus, they spent the next several months pushing their generals further and further toward this goal. Since the Russians ultimately got there first, when the victorious Allies met in Potsdam in 1945, it remained Britain and America's task to convince Stalin to divide the country, and even the city of Berlin, between them. They ultimately accomplished this, but at a terrible cost: Russia acquired the previously liberated Austria.

With the race toward Berlin in full throttle, General Dwight D. Eisenhower's Allied armies were within 200 miles of the city, but his biggest battles now took place among his allies, as he now had to deal diplomatically with Churchill, Montgomery, and French war hero Charles de Gaulle. After crossing the Rhine River, General George Patton advised Eisenhower to make haste for Berlin, and British General Bernard Montgomery was confident that they could reach Berlin before the Soviets, but Eisenhower did not think it "worth the trouble".[4] Eisenhower's forces went on to capture 400,000 prisoners on April 1st in the Ruhr, but despite his success there, not everyone agreed with Eisenhower's decision, especially Winston Churchill. In Churchill's thinking, the decision to leave the taking of Berlin to the Soviets would leave lasting trouble on the European continent, a more pressing concern for the British than for Americans an ocean away. In tension-filled exchanges, Churchill made his position clear, but President Roosevelt was ill and had no stomach for angering the Soviets. For his part, Eisenhower saw his role as a purely military one, so he refused to "trespass" into political arenas that he was under the impression had been worked out at the Tehran and Yalta conferences. In fact, Roosevelt had promised Stalin that he could enter Berlin despite the obvious threat to postwar security for the European countries, and Eisenhower wanted to avoid being a pawn in the political maneuverings of the three leaders. As a result, his major concern was to avoid as many casualties as possible in the coming weeks of the war, and if the Russians were prepared to attack and had the better opportunity to do so, it would save lives of American soldiers who would otherwise have to fight their way in from the west.[5] Eisenhower did not share his peers' (Patton and Montgomery, specifically) concerns of "arriving victorious in Berlin on top of a tank."[6]

Eventually, Eisenhower made the fateful choice not to move the American forces toward Berlin but to "hold a firm front on the Elbe" instead. In making this decision, Eisenhower left Berlin's capture to the Soviet army, and his decisions have been the cause of much debate ever since. The Allied armies in the west would thus concentrate on encircling the Ruhr Valley, the center of Germany's industry, instead of competing with the Soviets for control of the city.

---

[4] World War II: A 50th Anniversary History. New York: Holt, 1989.288.
[5] Humes, James C. Eisenhower and Churchill: The Partnership that Saved the World. Crown Publishing Group, 2010.
[6] Ibid.

Eisenhower

There were many concerns about the Soviet Union reaching Berlin, and all of them were understandable. Most people, especially the Germans, expected far worse treatment from Soviet conquerors than the British or Americans, especially since Hitler's attack on the Soviet Union (Operation Barbarossa) had been so unexpected that it stunned even Stalin into temporary inaction. Hitler and the Germans were going to pay dearly for the treatment that the Russians, both civilians and soldiers, had received at the hands of the German armies. Furthermore, the fear of a Soviet strategic advantage in Europe, anchored by a Soviet-controlled Berlin, loomed over both eastern and western European nations. Lastly, even if Stalin kept his word about the division of post-war Germany, allowing him unchallenged control was viewed as dangerous to a world with a weakened Britain and a United States looking to return to the isolation the Atlantic Ocean had previously provided.

Churchill and Roosevelt had always disagreed on Stalin's real motivations and limits, and

Churchill needed to maintain strong ties to the Americans as the war came to a close. During one of the meetings between the three, Stalin suggested that once the German armies had been defeated, 50,000 soldiers should be executed by the conquering armies in vengeance for the losses Germany had inflicted on Europe. That suggestion horrified Churchill, who stormed out of the meeting, but Stalin followed to assure Churchill that all that had been said was in jest. Churchill had very little choice but to take Stalin at his word, but he was always far more cautious than Roosevelt when it came to trust in Stalin's judgment or word. In any case, he wrote a letter to Roosevelt after his exchange with Eisenhower in March in which he said, "I wish to place on record the complete confidence felt by His Majesty's government in General Eisenhower and our pleasure that our armies are serving under his command and our admiration of his great and shining quality, character, and personality".[7] In a note he added to Eisenhower's copy of the letter, he expressed it would grieve him to know he had pained Eisenhower with his comments but still suggested that "we should shake hands with the Russians as far east as possible."[8]

By April 17, in a meeting between Eisenhower and Churchill, the fact that the Soviet army was positioned just over 30 miles from Berlin with overpowering men, artillery, and tanks convinced Churchill that the decision to allow the Soviets to lead the attack on the city was necessary. It is important to keep in perspective that Roosevelt's death just 5 days earlier likely played a role in Churchill's willingness to give in. Churchill had spent several years negotiating with both Stalin and Roosevelt, and he may have felt that time would not allow for further discussion on the matter. Eisenhower also was under pressure to end the war in Europe as soon as possible so that American forces and attention could be directed toward the fight against Japan. The campaign in Okinawa had just started and would last until June, and the extent of the carnage there made clear that Japan had no intention of surrendering anytime soon.

---

[7] Ibid.
[8] Ibid.

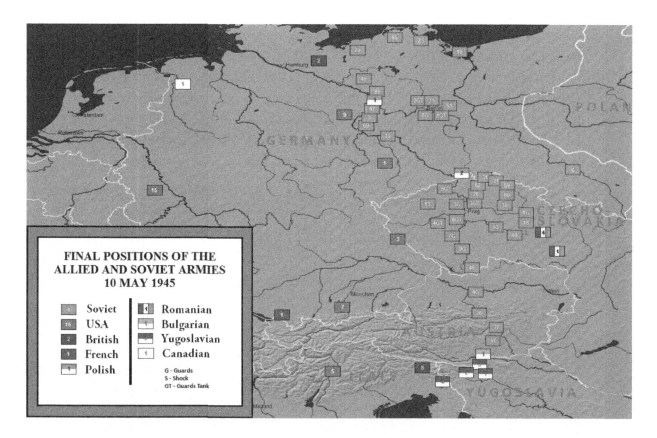

The lines at the end of World War II

The Battle of Berlin ended with an inevitable Soviet triumph, but by the time Germany officially surrendered, the Soviets had suffered over 350,000 casualties and had lost thousands of artillery batteries and armored vehicles. The Germans had suffered upwards of 100,000 dead and over 200,000 wounded, not to mention the horrors visited upon the civilian population in the wake of the battle.

With the fighting mostly coming to an end on May 2, the chain of German surrenders in the field outside of Berlin took off like dominoes. Field Marshal Wilhelm Keitel signed Germany's unconditional surrender on May 7, and news of the final surrender of the Germans was celebrated as Victory in Europe (V-E) day on May 8, 1945. Churchill delivered the following remarks to cheering crowds:

> "My dear friends, this is your hour. This is not victory of a party or of any class. It's a victory of the great British nation as a whole. We were the first, in this ancient island, to draw the sword against tyranny. After a while we were left all alone against the most tremendous military power that has been seen. We were all alone for a whole year.
>
> There we stood, alone. Did anyone want to give in? Were we down-hearted? The lights went out and the bombs came down. But every man, woman and child in the

country had no thought of quitting the struggle. London can take it. So we came back after long months from the jaws of death, out of the mouth of hell, while all the world wondered. When shall the reputation and faith of this generation of English men and women fail? I say that in the long years to come not only will the people of this island but of the world, wherever the bird of freedom chirps in human hearts, look back to what we've done and they will say 'do not despair, do not yield to violence and tyranny, march straightforward and die if need be-unconquered.'"

Bundesarchiv, Bild 183-R77799
Foto: o.Ang. | 8. Mai 1945

Pictures of the Germans' unconditional surrender on May 7

Of course, the announcement of surrender was met with a far different emotion among the Germans, as one Berliner remembered: "The next day, General Wilding, the commander of the German troops in Berlin, finally surrendered the entire city to the Soviet army. There was no radio or newspaper, so vans with loudspeakers drove through the streets ordering us to cease all resistance. Suddenly, the shooting and bombing stopped and the unreal silence meant that one ordeal was over for us and another was about to begin. Our nightmare had become a reality. The entire three hundred square miles of what was left of Berlin were now completely under control of the Red Army. The last days of savage house to house fighting and street battles had been a human slaughter, with no prisoners being taken on either side. These final days were hell. Our last remaining and exhausted troops, primarily children and old men, stumbled into imprisonment. We were a city in ruins; almost no house remained intact."

The controversy over Eisenhower's decision not to press for Berlin remains, but any debate over whether the Allied armies were in a position to take Berlin must acknowledge the fact that the most significant American forces were over 200 miles from Berlin in mid-April.

Nonetheless, others point to smaller American forces that were within 50 miles of the city before being told to move in the opposite direction.

The strongest critiques of Eisenhower's decisions portray him as naïve about the consequences, or as an unwitting tool of the Soviets, but his defenders call his decision "dead on".[9] Soviet casualties in taking the city rivaled those lost by the Allies at the Battle of the Bulge, and considering the earlier agreements with Stalin, General Omar Bradley believed that the Americans would have to pay "a pretty stiff price to pay for a prestige objective, especially when we've got to fall back and let the other fellow take over."[10]

Eisenhower vigorously defended himself against criticism upon his return from the war, pointing out that those who criticized his position on the issue were not the ones who would have been forced to comfort the grieving mothers of soldiers killed in an unnecessary fight to take Berlin. During his 1952 presidential campaign, he faced further criticism, and in response, he emphasized his warnings about the danger of the Soviet threat to Europe rather than discuss his decision to stay away from Berlin. Historian Stephen Ambrose saw this attempt at self-salvation by Eisenhower as wishful thinking, and that there was no evidence of Eisenhower warning against the Soviet threat to Europe during his time as general: "The truth was that he may have wished by 1952 that he had taken a hard line with the Russians in 1945, but he had not".[11]

---

[9] Kevin Baker, "General Discontent: Blaming Powell-And Eisenhower-For Not Having Pushed Through. (in the News)," American Heritage, November-December 2002, https://www.questia.com/read/1G1-93611493.
[10] Ibid.
[11] Ibid.

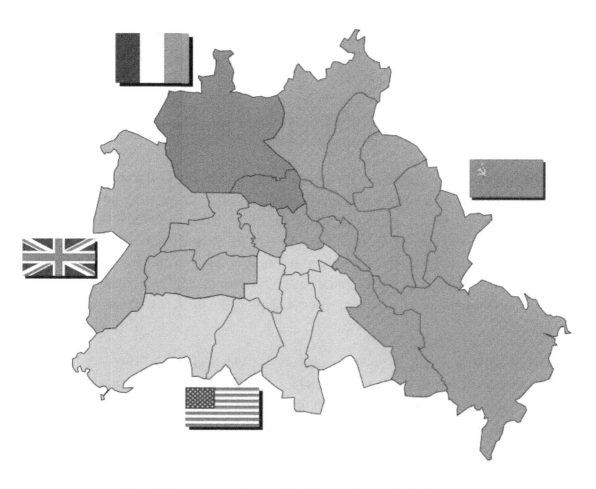

The different sections of Berlin at the end of the war

It was a famous moment commemorated as "East Meets West" when Soviet soldiers shook hands with other Allied soldiers in Germany near the end of the war, but nobody was under any illusions that they would continue to work well together after defeating their common enemy. In 1946, speaking to a war-weary world, Winston Churchill sounded what would become a famous warning about the aggression of the Soviet Union and the dangers of communism's spread while speaking to a group of college students at Westminster College in Fulton, Missouri: "I am sure you would wish me to state the facts as I see them to you, to place before you certain facts about the present position in Europe. From Stettin in the Baltic to Trieste in the Adriatic, an iron curtain has descended across the Continent. Behind that line lie all the capitals of the ancient states of Central Europe and Eastern Europe. Warsaw, Berlin, Prague, Vienna, Budapest, Belgrade, Bucharest and Sofia, all these famous cities and the populations around them lie in what I must call the Soviet sphere, and all are subject in one form or another, not only to Soviet influence but to a very high and, in many cases, increasing measure of control from Moscow."[12]

---

[12] Churchill, Winston. "The Sinews of Peace." Westminster College. Mississippi, Fulton. 5 Mar. 1946. *The Churchill Center*. Web. 2 Feb. 2015.

This "border" of states, the protection that Stalin claimed he needed to ensure his country's post-war security, included "Poland, Czechoslovakia, Hungary, Bulgaria, Romania, and the Soviet Occupation Zone in East Germany".[13] These areas would develop into Soviet satellite states, relying on the Soviet's for military defense, serving as the Soviet industrial plans' source for natural resources, and experiencing occasional crackdowns for showing signs of independence or unrest over the next 40 plus years.

At the same time, in the immediate aftermath of the war, the city of Berlin itself was divided into a French, British, American, and Soviet occupation zone. As on historian describes it, the division was uneven from the beginning: "[T]he victorious Allies unfurled a map and carved up the city - the houses then lining the south side of Bernauer Strasse wound up in the Soviet sector while the street itself and the sidewalk in front belonged to the French. By this cartographic fiat, some sectors of the population would find themselves economically rejuvenated by the Marshall Plan and reintroduced to bourgeois democratic society, while the rest were stuck with the Soviets.[14]

The city of Berlin was fully in Soviet hands between May and July of 1945, but they turned over the sectors they had agreed to back in 1944 to the British, Americans, and French. That said, in recognition of the last two months of the war, in which the Soviets had fought the Battle for Berlin at the cost of over 80,000 Soviet lives, the Soviets were given a much larger portion of the city than the rest of the Allies,[15] and as Germany divided into East and West along the borders of former German states, the city of Berlin ultimately fell well within East Germany's borders. In fact, Berlin was over 100 miles from the nearest point in what would become known as West Germany.

General Georgy Zhukov, the Soviet hero of the war, established the communist party in Berlin,[16] and the decisions governing Soviet action became immediately political, despite their desire to be seen (by both sides) as purely motivated by military necessity. At first, the city was governed by an "Allied Control Council" of the four powers, with each country rotating control on a monthly basis. In *City on Leave: A History of Berlin 1945-1962*, Philip Windsor explains that the council was marked far more for argument and conflict than true governance. In fact, he argues, "All the Western Powers were…for different reasons, convinced that collaboration with the Soviet Union in Germany was their essential task. The struggle for the country came upon them almost unawares, and at the outset none was capable of answering the scarcely defined Russian threat. This threat would not become manifest until they were all forced to face the need of defining common economic policies and erecting a central German authority. But there was

---

[13] Rottman, 5.
[14] Mark Ehrman, "Borders and Barriers," The Virginia Quarterly Review 83, no. 2 (2007), https://www.questia.com/read/1P3-1256577881.
[15] Ibid., 8.
[16] Philip Windsor, City on Leave: A History of Berlin, 1945-1962 (London: Chatto & Windus, 1963), 25, https://www.questia.com/read/11076907.

already one center in Germany where all were concerned together in a common assignation, and where the present government of the country was established. It offered a valuable, perhaps decisive, prize to Russia in the political conquest of the whole; and in the Rooseveltian terms which governed American policy, it provided the United States with the most practical test of Soviet intentions. *This was Berlin.*"[17]

Zhukov

In the early years of the Cold War, the West seemed to be in retreat as the Soviet Union succeeded in testing its own nuclear weapon, setting up puppet states in eastern Europe, and

---

[17] Ibid, 31. Emphasis added.

assisting the Chinese communists in winning a civil war over Western backed Chinese nationalist forces. Stalin subsequently hoped to continue to expand Russian influence by ordering a blockade of all supplies into West Berlin, hoping the West would cede the entire city to the Soviets. However, the United States and its allies were able to organize a massive airlift of supplies that kept the city of West Berlin supplied, and the Soviet Union and its German allies eventually stopped the blockade when they realized the West could continue to supply Berlin by air indefinitely. The Berlin Airlift was one of the first major confrontations of the Cold War, but it would hardly be the last; if anything, it was just the start for the contest over Berlin.

Picture of a plane participating in the Berlin Airlift in 1948

The ideological battle being played out in Berlin and greater Germany was fought between two spheres of influence led by the United States and the Soviet Union, but in the midst of the fight were the Germans, the people who had to live under the outcomes of policy, negotiations, and compromises formed by the push and pull of politics. Both sides of the conflict acknowledged that if the situation in Berlin ever required the use of nuclear weapons, the loss of German life would be devastating.

German leadership on both sides was required to maintain a delicate balance of working with the United States in the case of the West and the Soviets in the case of the East, as well as representing the interests and outcomes of their own people. For this reason, local leaders also played crucial roles in the division of Berlin and the construction of the wall.

Willy Brandt was the mayor of West Berlin from 1957-1966, and though he went on to serve as German chancellor and leader of a major German political party, it is for his time as mayor that he is best remembered. Brandt was a left-wing socialist who fled Germany during the Nazi reign, spending time in Scandinavia, but during the time of the Spanish Civil War, he came to distrust the Soviet Union and to champion the causes of German socialism rather than cooperation with the Soviet Union.

Brandt and Kennedy

As mayor of West Berlin, Brandt became the face for a group of over two million people whose lives hung in the balance of big decision-makers. President Kennedy invited Brandt to the White House in March 1961, and the English-speaking Brandt made a great impression on the young president. Kennedy hoped that he would be elected Chancellor of Germany in the next months, a desire that actually caused tension between Kennedy and the actual future chancellor.[18]

The future leader of communist East Germany began as a member of the Communist Party of Germany. Fleeing to Russia during the Nazi domination, Walter Ulbricht rose to power in Stalin's circles, supporting the purges and staying out of trouble. He returned to Germany as part of the Soviet occupation in 1945 and became the head of a new party, the Socialist Unity Party, which would control East Germany.[19] Ulbricht has been characterized by history as both a communist radical who pressured the Soviets into the construction of the wall, and as a leader more interested in independence and reforms that would move his country in a different direction than the other Soviet bloc nations.

Ulbricht and Khrushchev

Konrad Adenauer was the first chancellor of Germany. Having been a prisoner of war under the Nazi regime, he was named the mayor of Berlin the day after the conclusion of the war, but the British dismissed him from this position. He formed the Christian Democratic Union party, which was anti-Socialist but concerned with the poor who had been devastated by Germany's

---

[18] Kempe, Frederick. "West Berlin's Impertinent Mayor". *Reuters Blog: Analysis and Opinion*. 7 June 2011.
[19] Dennis Kavanagh, ed., A Dictionary of Political Biography (Oxford: Oxford University Press, 1998), 484, https://www.questia.com/read/34683386.

economic hard times. Adenauer believed that friendliness with the United States, Britain, and France was necessary in order to protect Berlin and West Germany itself from the Soviets.[20]

Adenauer

With tensions between the West and East high, Germany officially became two countries in 1949. West Germany was founded on May 23, 1949, and four months later, on October 7, the German Democratic Republic (DDR, from the German: *Deutsche Demokratische Republik*) – East Germany to non-Germans – officially came into existence. The Eastern half was closely

---

[20] Dennis Kavanagh, ed., A Dictionary of Political Biography (Oxford: Oxford University Press, 1998), 4, https://www.questia.com/read/34683386.

linked to the Soviet government and rejected the existence of West Germany, claiming East Germany was "the only legal German state, to which the future of Germany belongs."[21]

Naturally, elections in the 1940s did not lead to a vibrant democracy, and when the Soviets handed control over to the SED government, the country was well on its way to Stalinization. An overbearing surveillance and state security apparatus denied basic freedoms to its citizens. The much-feared Stasi (State Security Service or *Staatssicherheitsdienst*) was formed in 1950. For his part, Ulbricht dreamed of building an East Germany that could compete with the West, instituting 5 year plans and insisting that "[t]he victory of the working people over the exploiters and slave holders is at the same time the victorious struggle for liberation by the German people".

Most historians agree that the German Democratic Republic was little more than a puppet state of the Soviet Union, especially during the early years of its existence. It is also true that the Federal Republic of Germany was not a sovereign nation until 10 years after the conclusion of the war. The Allies, led by the Americans, negotiated with West German authorities to reinstate the sovereignty of West Germany.

In the midst of this in 1952, Stalin came forward with a "peace note" offering to reorganize Germany and unite it as a neutral nation, but the West considered this nothing more than timely propaganda designed to cause division within West Germany about accepting the terms of the Allies for recognition of West Germany as an independent state. Stalin suggested not that the countries be united, but that West Germany gain her independence and not become a member of any western alliance. The Allies, as well as many West Germans, did not believe they could trust the Soviets to respect West Germany's neutrality and stated that the time for negotiation with Stalin had passed. American foreign policymakers such as Henry Kissinger also suggested that a neutral Germany would have to be very heavily armed in order to defend herself in the midst of Europe, especially with the Soviet satellite states all along her border. Since "a strong, unified Germany in the center of the continent pursuing purely national policy had proved incompatible with the peace of Europe[22]", this could not be an acceptable solution.

In 1952, the Inner German Border between East and West Germany was constructed by the East German government, and from then on, "the inner-German border became one of Cold War Europe's most menacing frontiers—an 858-mile death-strip of barbed wire fences, control points, watchtowers, mines, and, later, automatic shooting devices".[23] It is important to remember that while the rate of deaths for those attempting to cross the Berlin Wall between 1961 and 1989 is often estimated to be about 200, nearly another 700 East Germans were killed crossing the Inner German border during the same period.[24]

---

[21] Ibid. 11.
[22] Wilke, Manfred. The Path to the Berlin Wall: Critical Stages in the History of Divided Germany. New York: Berghahn Books, 2014.88.
[23] David Clay Large, *Berlin* (New York: Basic Books, 2000), 425, https://www.questia.com/read/100504423.

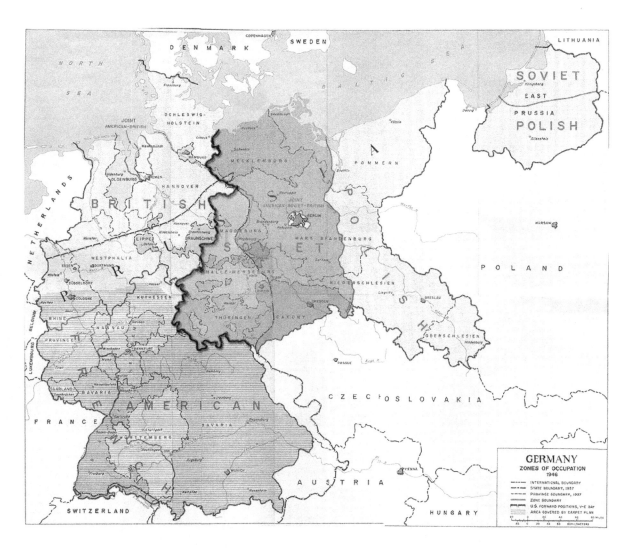

The route of the border in black

---

[24] Jim Willis, Daily Life behind the Iron Curtain (Santa Barbara, CA: Greenwood, 2013), 113

Pictures of various sections of the Inner German border

In an attempt to control the people of East Berlin and avoid contact with Westerners, Ulbricht worked to isolate East Berliners. Berlin historian David Clay Large notes that by 1952, East Germany was already feeling the effects of failed agricultural collectivization schemes, extreme production quotas, the nationalization of major industry, and neglect of consumer goods. After the Inner German border's completion in 1952, East Germans could only leave for the west through the city of Berlin, but they continued to do so in droves, with over 130,000 leaving in just the second half of 1952 and the first 3 months of 1953. Ironically, instead of changing or moderating some of the demands the government was making on East German workers, Ulbricht upped production quotas to even higher levels.[25]

After West Germany regained sovereignty as an independent nation in 1955, it signed the North Atlantic Treaty and became a member of NATO. NATO member nations delivered a declaration to the effect that "They consider the government of the Federal Republic as the only German government freely and legitimately constituted and therefore entitled to speak for

---

[25] David Clay Large, *Berlin* (New York: Basic Books, 2000), 425, https://www.questia.com/read/100504423.

Germany as the representative of the German people in international affairs."[26]

Meanwhile, by 1955, East Germany was attempting to combat the "brain drain" directly through propaganda messages to the East German people. According to the Eastern Bloc, those who desired to leave the communist state were being fooled by capitalist propaganda and puppets of the western fascists:

> "In both from the moral standpoint as well as in terms of the interests of the whole German nation, leaving the GDR is an act of political and moral backwardness and depravity. Those who let themselves be recruited objectively serve West German Reaction and militarism, whether they know it or not. Is it not despicable when for the sake of a few alluring job offers or other false promises about a "guaranteed future" one leaves a country in which the seed for a new and more beautiful life is sprouting, and is already showing the first fruits, for the place that favours a new war and destruction?
>
> Is it not an act of political depravity when citizens, whether young people, workers, or members of the intelligentsia, leave and betray what our people have created through common labour in our republic to offer themselves to the American or British secret services or work for the West German factory owners, Junkers, or militarists? Does not leaving the land of progress for the morass of an historically outdated social order demonstrate political backwardness and blindness? ...[W]orkers throughout Germany will demand punishment for those who today leave the German Democratic Republic, the strong bastion of the fight for peace, to serve the deadly enemy of the German people, the imperialists and militarists."[27]

An indication of just how bad conditions got is that the Soviets began to advise Ulbricht to ease off of collectivization and production quotas. The Soviets were becoming embarrassed by the mass defections to the west and feared that if protests were to arise in East Germany, they could spread to other communist regimes, or even the Soviet Union itself. However, for political reasons, Ulbricht refused; he had seen the results for others who had not followed a hard line approach in the past, and he believed the best way to save himself was to continue to demand more from the East German people. Thus, in defiance of the Soviets, he increased quotas by an additional 25 percent.

Finally, a group of construction workers began an informal strike that spread quickly and grew out of control in a matter of days. With the world watching, the Soviets knew they had to act

---

[26] Wilke, Manfred. The Path to the Berlin Wall: Critical Stages in the History of Divided Germany. New York: Berghahn Books, 2014.87.

[27] ("He Who Leaves the German Democratic Republic Joins the Warmongers", Notizbuch des Agitators ("Agitator's Notebook"), Berlin: Socialist Unity Party's Agitation Department, November 1955.

quickly to leave no question about what would happen if communist authority were questioned. Soviet tanks rolled into East Berlin and the East German secret police were unleashed on the people. In the immediate clash, over 200 were killed, and almost 5,000 were arrested. The uprising, though embarrassing to the Soviets, likely guaranteed Ulbricht would remain in power despite his disobedience so that any appearance of "giving into protests" might be avoided.[28]

One historian sees the lack of action on the part of the various forces in Berlin as an important lesson for the USSR in the future. By not intervening in the violent response to East German protests, "what the Western Allies seemed to be saying was that the Soviets and GDR authorities had carte blanche in East Berlin, so long as they did not try to push the Western powers out of West Berlin. It was a message that the Soviets, the GDR government, and most of all the East German people, would not soon forget".[29]

The Birth of the Stasi

From its earliest days, East Germany's economy stagnated, falling further and further behind its western neighbor, though this was not self-evident at the time. However, East Germany had a number of advantages as well, most notably the fact that it had suffered less bomb damage than the West and had a solid industrial base. Nevertheless, supply chains the region had relied upon before the Nazis' surrender had been cut off after the war. Crucially, East Germany contained only 2% of Germany's total coal deposits.[30] It was also more sparsely populated than West Germany and the Soviet zone, and its successor state hemorrhaged people at shockingly high rates, seeing over 100,000 East Germans leave for the West each year during 1951, 1952, and 1953, despite the only legitimate route being the Berlin corridor.[31]

By far the most important factor in the divergence between the two countries was governance and economic management. Nazi Germany had been a highly repressive state. A number of competing agencies, including the Sturmabteilung (SA), Schutzstaffel (SS) and Gestapo, had strangled free expression, locked up opponents of the regime, and kept watch on its citizens. Most notably, the Nazi security services pursued Hitler's racial and anti-Semitic policies with brutal efficiency. In this respect the Stasi was a continuation of the totalitarian policies of its predecessors, but there was also a uniquely communist and Stalinist dimension to the Stasi. The Soviet Union never commanded majority support for its communist agenda. As a result, Soviet authorities, particularly under Stalin, attempted to impose obedience and monitor potential dissenters. In reality this meant a secret police, the KGB, political prisoners and labor camps: the Gulag. This model was repeated throughout the communist world, as more and more countries

---

[28] Ibid. 429-430.
[29] Ibid.
[30] Giles MacDonogh, *After the Reich : from the fall of Vienna to the Berlin airlift* (London: John Murray, 2007), p. 202
[31] Christian Ostermann, *Uprising in East Germany, 1953 : the Cold War, the German question, and the first major upheaval behind the Iron Curtain* (Budapest: Central European Press, 2001), p. 3.

adopted centralized socialist dictatorships during the twentieth century. It was one of the core contradictions within communist rule, that regimes supposedly formed to better human development often endorsed inhumane treatment and surveillance of potential – and often imagined - adversaries.

From the beginning, the occupying Soviet forces were keen to set up a communist administration in Berlin. In the early months after 1945, a Soviet Military Administration in Germany (SMAD) took control, and the following year elections were held. The communists were popular and the KPD (German: Kommunist Partei Deutschlands) won a significant proportion of the vote. Nevertheless, it was not enough for a meaningful mandate as the socialist party, and the more moderate SPD (German: Sozialist Partei Deutschlands), also proved popular. The SMAD then forced a merger of the SPD and KPD, establishing the SED (Socialist Unity Party). Initially the SED had a joint SPD-KPD leadership of Otto Grotewoahl and Wilhelm Pieck, between 1946 and 1950. The KPD detested the Social Democrats, however, and soon assumed complete control of the SED. Insecurity over its popularity and therefore legitimacy therefore haunted the SED, which ruled the DDR throughout its existence. This anxiety partly explains the rise of the Stasi. In fact the SED began to imprison opponents almost immediately, and an early version of the secret police was formed in the late 1940s.

The Stasi - or Ministry for State Security (MfS) - was formed on February 8, 1950, after a law was passed by the DDR's parliament, the Volkskammer, effectively a rubberstamp chamber for the SED. The Stasi's motto became the SED's "shield and sword." The Ministry was sold to the East German population as a defensive measure, in order to repel Western subversion. The Soviet authorities had a genuine (and justified) fear that Allied agents were operating in the communist zone during the late 1940s and this was one stimulus for the new institution. What is perhaps surprising, however, is that it took so long for the DDR authorities to form a secret police. This may have been due to the reluctance the Soviets had in granting East Germany its own institutions; the USSR was suspicious both of the West, as 1950 was a particularly tense moment in the fledgling Cold War, and more generally of the Germans, even communist ones.[32]

Wilhelm Zaisser was appointed the first head of the MfS in 1950. He shared an experience in common with several other East German leaders: the Spanish Civil War. What started out as a 1936 army coup against the Spanish Republic descended into a conflict between German and Italian-backed fascists and Soviet-backed communists. Supporting the latter was a multinational force of volunteers, the International Brigades. Zaisser was a leading figure in the International Brigades, known by the nom de guerre General Gomez.[33] He had been a long-term member of the KPD and had resisted the infamous right-wing Putsch of 1920, later serving time in prison.

---

[32] David Childs and Richard Popplewell, *The Stasi: The East German Intelligence and Security Service* (New York: New York University Press, 1996), pp. 41, 46.
[33] Mike Dennis, *The Rise and Fall of the German Democratic Republic 1945-1990* (Harlow: Longman, 2000), p. 35.

Zaisser

Zaisser's right-hand man in Spain was Erich Mielke.[34] They were joined in the conflict by Ernst Wollweber and Walter Ulbricht.[35] All became leading figures in the DDR's security apparatus, and Ulbricht was the state's first leader. One feature of the communist forces in Spain was the internecine rivalry between different left-wing factions. These German communists were involved in implementing "discipline" within the relatively heterogeneous ranks. It has been reported that Ulbricht, in particular, vigorously helped track down Trotskyist elements in Spain and had them purged and even killed.[36] Therefore the key players within the DDR and the Stasi already displayed some of their key features and practices well in advance of the MfS' formation in 1950.

---

[34] David Childs and Richard Popplewell, *The Stasi: The East German Intelligence and Security Service* (New York: New York University Press, 1996), pp. 24, 47.
[35] Ibid, p. 28.
[36] Ibid, p. 27.

Mielke

The Stasi was given free rein to achieve its objectives of preventing subversion within the DDR and thus had few legal restrictions.[37] The MfS inherited the structures of the pre-DDR security system and once it had been founded, was a key tool in maintaining the SED's total control over the country.[38] It was an amalgamation of the departments of intelligence and information, the criminal police and the office of political culture.[39] The MfS itself had a complex and multipronged organizational structure of main departments, sub-departments, a reconnaissance administration and other working groups and sectors. Each was given a label such as XX or XVII.[40] Much of the notorious infrastructure was put in place in this early period. For instance, the Stasi inherited the Berlin-Hohenschönhausen camp in 1951[41] and became one of its two detention and interrogation centers.[42]

---

[37] Ibid, p. 47.
[38] Peter Pulzer, *German Politics, 1945-1995* (Oxford: Oxford University Press, 1995), p. 94.
[39] Mike Dennis, *The Rise and Fall of the German Democratic Republic 1945-1990* (Harlow: Longman, 2000), p. 35.
[40] Mike Dennis, *The Rise and Fall of the German Democratic Republic 1945-1990* (Harlow: Longman, 2000), p. 216.
[41] 'Stasi Prison', Gedenkstätte Berlin-Hohenschönhausen, [accessed 5 January 2018], http://www.stiftung-hsh.de/history/stasi-prison/
[42] Mike Dennis, *The Rise and Fall of the German Democratic Republic 1945-1990* (Harlow: Longman, 2000), p. 36.

The Formation of the KGB

During the Great Patriotic War (the term the Soviets used to refer to the fighting against Nazi Germany during World War II), scientific, political, and military intelligence exerted a great influence on Soviet politics, and the NKVD played a crucial role. According to Soviet estimates, the NKVD had 53 divisions and 28 brigades, "not counting the many independent units and border troops" (Gordievskiy and Andru, 1992), many of which were used as security units to prevent the escape of troops and to carry out punitive operations against "unreliable peoples." A number of minorities, including Chechens, Ingush, Crimean Tatars, Karachais, Balkars, Kalmyks, and Volga Germans, were victims of NKVD mass killings and forced evictions.

In March 1946, the NKGB and NKVD were transformed from commissariats to ministries, which meant raising their status. Later, they were known as the Ministry of State Security (MGB) and the Ministry of Internal Affairs (MVD), respectively. Viktor Semenovich Abakumov became the head of the MGB. Stalin had expected that Abakumov would limit Beria's influence in the state security agencies, but he was wrong, and Abakumov quickly became a "trusted person of Beria." (ibid). In fact, he never reported to anyone, not even Stalin, without first consulting Beria.

Abakumov's leadership style was marked by cruelty and corruption, but he was friendly and kind with his protégés. In all likelihood, Abakumov was the one who was sensitive about being in the shadow of the Cheka and thus ordered previously sacred relics removed from the memorial room in the officer's club of the MGB. Most notably, Dzerzhinsky's death mask and portrait were removed, and a tradition was established in which officers of the MGB who had traveled abroad expressed their respect to Abakumov with expensive gifts. Immoral behavior and corruption were mentioned among the official reasons for Abakumov's arrest in 1951 and his subsequent execution in 1954.

After World War II, the Soviet Union recognized the United States as its "main enemy." Great Britain, the main object of NKVD interests before the war, became a secondary concern. During the war, when the Soviet Union found itself allied with the U.S. and the British, Russian intelligence was working in the West with less interference than ever before, but once the war ended and the Cold War dawned, Moscow faced new problems. The first, oddly enough, was the demobilization of American and British intelligence units. The decision by President Truman to liquidate the Office of Strategic Services (the predecessor of the CIA) in September 1945 deprived the NKGB and many of their agents of the possibility of penetration into their main enemy's secret services. After the establishment of the Central Intelligence Agency (CIA) in 1947, Soviet intelligence had to start from scratch. Moreover, their penetration into the CIA was much more difficult than penetration into the OSS had been.

By the time the CIA was created in July 1947, many effective verification methods had become widely used that made the introduction of Soviet agents impossible. Soviet intelligence services would be able to inflict the greatest damage on American intelligence via the interception and decipherment of classified intelligence.

While Moscow retained intelligence forces in the West, the West did not have the same opportunities in Moscow. Almost all attempts to penetrate Russia across the border from the Baltic in the north and Turkey in the south failed as a result of Moscow's counterintelligence operations.

The 1950s saw the death of Stalin, the brief stay in power of Beria, the rejection of Stalin's cult of personality by Nikita Khrushchev; the first political "thaw," and the birth of the KGB. Once its structure and principles of activity were formed, it remained mostly unchanged for almost 40 years.

The situation in America had also dynamically been changed. For example, in January 1956, under President Eisenhower's direction, a Council of Consultants was formed to periodically review intelligence issues abroad, and the intelligence apparatus of England was expanded. From 1955-1957, four new departments were created to work against socialist countries. In 1957-1958, a major reorganization of intelligence and counter-intelligence bodies of France was carried out.

One of the main reasons for the reforms was the need to carry out tasks arising from the countries' membership in NATO. On a semi-legal basis, the German intelligence service "The Organization of Gehlen" was included in the structure of the government bodies of West Germany until 1956. In contrast to the first post-war decade, when West Germany had led tactical reconnaissance in Hungary, the GDR, and Czechoslovakia, it now began conducting reconnaissance operations in the territory of the Soviet Union.

After Stalin's death, there was a weakening of the repressive policy toward those who had cooperated with the German occupiers during the Great Patriotic War. In September 1955, the Decree of the Presidium of the Supreme Soviet of the USSR gave amnesty to this category of citizens. Former Soviet citizens who had found themselves abroad now returned to the country.

Between 1955 and 1958, over 12,000 people came home, and foreign special services hastened to use this "channel" to send agents to the Soviet Union. According to author Alexander Sever, "Since 1956, among the immigrants arriving in the USSR, operational officers exposed 30 to 50 foreign intelligence agents and emissaries of anti-Soviet centers and organizations every year. In particular, in 1957, 26 agents of the imperialist intelligence services and 36 participants of foreign anti-Soviet centers and organizations were found among the arriving immigrants."

Not only did the Russian intelligence services have to fight with the external enemies of the Soviet state, they also had to deal with internal enemies, such as "Banderaers" and "forest brothers" who had cooperated with the German invaders. After the Red Army had liberated the territory of Western Ukraine, Belarus, and the Baltic States, they began to terrorize and plunder the local civilian population.

According to the Resolution of the Central Committee of the Communist Party (CPSU) of March 12, 1954, the main operational activities of state security agencies in the latter 1950s included the struggle against destructive activities of the imperialist intelligence services and foreign anti-Soviet centers, the elimination of the remnants of the "bourgeois-nationalist underground" in the territories of Western Ukraine, Belorussia, and the Baltic republics, and the struggle against anti-Soviet elements, such as churchmen, sectarians, and other hostile elements within the country (Sever, 2008). By the beginning of the 1960s, the Soviets had only managed the second task of eliminating the remnants of the "bourgeois-nationalist underground."

The 1950s were also recognized in the Soviet Union as a "period of reforms and reductions." From 1953-1967, the Soviet Union had five leaders, structural and functional changes took place regularly, and massive staff cuts were made. The Central Committee of the CPSU began the process of transforming state security on July 11, 1951, due to " the unfavorable situation in the Ministry of State Security of the USSR." Two days later, the Minister of the MGB, General Viktor Abakumov, lost his position and was arrested. He was replaced by former secretary of the Central Committee of the CPSU, Semyon Ignatiev. The change of the head of the department subsequently led to a series of resignations in the central apparatus and in territorial bodies.

In January 1952, a system of secret informants was eliminated and a new category of special agents was introduced. That November, the Bureau of the Presidium of the CPSU Central Committee also established a commission to reorganize the intelligence and counter-intelligence services of the MGB USSR. As a result of its activities, the Bureau of the Presidium of the CPSU Central Committee adopted a decision (BP7 / 12-op of December 30, 1952) for the establishment of the Main Intelligence Directorate in the USSR MGB on January 5, 1953, by the order of MGB No. 006, but the project was never implemented due to the death of Stalin in March 1953.

New reforms began after that. At a joint meeting of the Plenum of the CPSU Central Committee, the Council of Ministers of the USSR and the Presidium of the Supreme Soviet of the USSR, a decision was made to merge the MGB and Ministry of Internal Affairs (Ministry of the Interior of the USSR). This move was initiated by Beria. At the same meeting, it was decided to appoint Beria as the First Deputy Chairman of the Council of Ministers of the USSR, and at the same time, Minister of the Interior of the USSR. He held these posts for a short time before being arrested on June 26, 1953, the result of an initiative undertaken by a "group of comrades from the Politburo." Beria was shot on December 23, 1953.

After Beria's arrest, Sergei Kruglov, the new Minister of Internal Affairs, filed an official note to the "instance" (the so-called Central Committee of the CPSU) on February 4, 1954, with a proposal to establish a "Committee for State Security under the Council Ministers of the USSR." This document was discussed on February 8, 1954, at the Presidium of the Central Committee of the CPSU, and fully approved.

The Committee for State Security ("Komitet Gosudarstvennoy Bezopasnosti" in Russian), was established in accordance with the Decree of the Presidium of the Supreme Soviet of the USSR of March 13, 1954. This date is considered the official date of the KGB's birth, although the Chekists mark the holiday on December 20, the day of the Cheka's creation.

Ivan Serov was appointed the first chairman of the KGB. He had risen rapidly in his career under Stalin and Khrushchev, actively participated in the procedure of rehabilitation of victims of judicial arbitrariness, and by June 1957, had fired more than 18,000 security officers, including 40 generals.

Serov

This wave of personnel changes was completed in February 1956, when Serov "reported" the dismissal of 16,000 employees to the Central Committee of the CPSU "as politically not confiable, violators of socialist legality, careerists, morally unstable, as well as illiterate and backward workers."

The second stage of "cleansing" ended in June 1957, when another 2,000 employees of the central apparatus were dismissed from state security agencies "for violating Soviet legality, abuse of office and immoral acts." There were 48 people who held the posts of heads of departments and other higher positions. As a result, as noted in the certificate prepared by Serov for the (1957) Plenum of the Central Committee, "almost all senior officials of the central administrations, departments of the central apparatus were changed." (Lubyanka, 2003). As a result of personnel cuts, the number of State Security Committee workers decreased in 1957 by half compared to 1954. Moving forward, Serov would rely both on old Chekists and new party nominees.

Under Serov, the tasks and responsibilities of the KGB's central apparatus and its local bodies were clearly formulated:

    a) intelligence work in capitalist countries;
    b) combating espionage, sabotage, terrorist, and other subversive activities of foreign intelligence agencies, foreign anti-Soviet centers, and their agents inside the country;
    c) the struggle against anti-Soviet activities and nationalist elements within the USSR;
    d) counter-intelligence work in the Soviet Army, the Navy, GVF (Civil Air Fleet), border troops, and the troops of the Ministry of Interior in order to prevent the penetration of foreign intelligence agents and other enemy elements into their ranks;
    e) counter-intelligence work at special facilities and in the sphere of transport;
    f) state border protection of the USSR;
    g) protection of party and government leaders;
    h) organization and provision of government communications;
    i) the organization of radio-reconnaissance work; [and]
    j) [the] development of mobilization plans for the deployment of the state security organs and the military units of the Committee and the fulfilment of other assignments of the Central Committee of the CPSU and the Government of the USSR.

In this document, the rights of state security bodies were defined:

    a) to have necessary agents to conduct operational works in order to identify and suppress hostile activities directed against the Soviet Union;
    b) produce and legally establish searches, detentions and arrests of persons convicted or suspected of criminal activities;
    c) to conduct an investigation in cases of state crimes, committed by officers, sergeants, servants and workers of the KGB;
    d) to carry out special measures aimed at detecting the criminal activity of foreign intelligence agents and anti-Soviet elements;

    e)   in cases of necessity, in coordination with police chiefs, to involve the police in order to ensure the fulfilment of the tasks of state security bodies;

    f)   to keep operative records of state criminals and persons who are suspected of belonging to foreign intelligence agencies, participation in anti-Soviet organizations, and other hostile activities;

    g)   to check the state of the encryption service and secret records management in ministries and departments, as well as subordinate enterprises and institutions;

    h)   to carry out a special inspection of persons with careers in relation to state and military secrets, as well as those who go abroad and back to the USSR; [and]

    i)   publish literature, training, and visual aids on matters within the competence of the Committee (Shevyakin, 2004).

Over the course of its history, the activities of the KGB were regulated by more than 5,000 different normative acts approved by the Council of Ministers of the USSR. According to contemporaries of Serov, he was an agile, proactive, hard-working person who used to demand rapid decision-making from his subordinates. He listened to the opinion of famous scientists, retained departmental patriotism, and did not allow for further reduction of the central apparatus. The main reason for his resignation from his post as chairman of the KGB on December 8, 1958, was based on his complicated relationship with the USSR's highest party leadership.

The allocation of state security agencies to a separate department required the establishment of a special KGB award. Thus, on December 6, 1957, on the 40th anniversary of the bodies, a badge of the Honorary State Security Officer was established to be awarded "for the concrete results achieved in operational performance" in accordance with the decision of the board of the Committee.

After the reorganization of the Ministry of Internal Affairs and the formation of the KGB under the Council of Ministers of the USSR, counter-intelligence was renamed the Second Main Directorate of the KGB (VGU). At that point, security officers had to completely reorganize their work. If earlier foreign secret services actively used their agents in the territory of the Soviet Union through illegal channels, now they preferred legal means of "delivering" them to the territory of the Soviet Union. Naturally, the Soviets assumed the best place to find foreign spies would be among embassy employees, tourists, journalists, and businessmen. In 1955 and the first half of 1956, the Soviets exposed more than 40 foreign spies "among American, British, French and other delegation participants."

The sphere of interests had also been changed. Now, the object of their increased attention was the sphere of nuclear energy, the creation of hydrogen weapons, and rocketry. The wide use of the latest radio electronic equipment, pulsed radio navigation, and radar devices was used. By 1956, foreign intelligence had switched to one-way radio communication with its agents. Microphotography was also widely used. A popular way of contacting agents working under diplomatic cover in the territory of the Soviet Union was the use of systems of impersonal communication. All of this greatly complicated the identification of enemy agents.

In 1954, a strengthening of the intelligence apparatus was carried out, excluding agents who did not inspire confidence and who were incapable of assisting the KGB authorities with their personal qualities and counter-intelligence capabilities. In 1955, the KGB issued Order No. 00420, "On Improving Agency Work," which aimed "to recruit persons with higher and secondary education who possessed the necessary personal qualities and operational capabilities to conduct spy and other subversive activities, to search for state criminals and solve other counter-intelligence tasks" (Abramov, 2006).

In July 1954, the USSR Ministry of Foreign Affairs announced that Military Assistant and Attache of the U.S. Embassy in Moscow Howard Felchlin and Military Assistant and Attache of the US Embassy Major Walter McKinney were "persona non grata." These men traveled through the territory of the Soviet Union on a regular basis and were actively engaged in spying. During one trip, Felchlin and McKinney forgot espionage records denouncing their true activities in their train compartment. The next month, the USSR Ministry of Foreign Affairs sent protest notes to the U.S. Embassy in Moscow about the systematic attempts of the two men to penetrate the area of military facilities. In May 1955, the U.S. military assistants in Moscow, Colonel John Benson, Captain William Strode, and Captain Walter Mühle, were named "persona non grata" in connection with the fact they had made extensive trips to Soviet territory and were actively collecting spy information.

In January 1957, U.S. military assistants in Moscow Major Hubert Tensei and Captain Charles Stockel were also expelled from the Soviet Union after they allegedly made repeated attempts to penetrate areas where military units, airfields and other military facilities were located. In 1958, the Second Secretary of the U.S. Embassy was forced to leave, and in 1959, the First Secretary of the U.S. Embassy, David Mark, also left,

At the end of the 1950s, the CIA began to actively involve American scientists in the gathering of information about the Soviet Union's achievements and plans in the field of rocket science. They received intelligence data during meetings with Soviet colleagues in what the Americans called "Operation Lincoln." The operation, which came to involve over 100 people, was considered a partial success.

By 1963, the CIA would seek to collect information on every major development in Soviet science and technology, and the reaction of the KGB was immediate. Already in the early 1950s, American and British intelligence had undertaken a series of unsuccessful attempts to collect information on the Soviet nuclear industry. Most often, the collection of information was entrusted to agent-parachutists, but almost all of them were quickly identified and arrested without the time to get the information back. After Stalin's death and the partial weakening of the counter-intelligence regime, foreign diplomats increasingly began to participate in operations seeking to uncover Soviet atomic secrets. In this, NATO partners did not lag behind the United States. For example, British intelligence began to conduct "Operation Legal Traveler," with the main objective of collecting water and air samples to determine areas for testing nuclear weapons, as well as identifying objects associated with its production and storage, which involved English tourists, businessmen, and scientists who had legally entered the territory of the Soviet Union.

Suppressing the 1953 Uprising in East Germany

In its early phase, the Stasi relied on physical, often brutal methods to identify possible dissidents, but this began to change when Stalin died in 1953. That same year, the country erupted into a series of crises thanks to widespread protests, and the power struggle and attempts to shift blame for the uprisings culminated in the dismissal of Zaisser and the MfS developing its particular East German traits.

Zaisser had quickly built the Stasi into a formidable intelligence machine. His focus, however, had been on the infiltration of foreign agents.[43] The MfS had been caught by surprise regarding the extent of domestic unrest brewing by the summer of 1953. The "Berlin Uprising" that began that June became the first of several intermittent rebellions that occurred across Central and Eastern Europe until the communist system collapsed at the end of the 1980s. The DDR became a lodestar in the 1950s, just as it was to become in 1989. The major difference between these two points was that the Stasi took significant actions to prevent further uprisings, whereas in 1989 it had achieved what it believed was flächendeckend, complete coverage or surveillance.

As a power struggle to succeed Stalin ensued in Moscow, a debate opened up in the communist world over how best to run the system of a centralized economy. DDR leader Walter Ulbricht had tried to force through a program of collectivization. This calamitous move led to shortages for East Germans, who began to run out of basic goods, or at least have them rationed. The ire of DDR citizens was also aimed at the Stasi which had locked up scores of possible dissidents.[44] Meanwhile, new Soviet Premier Georgy Malenkov was advocating an economic "New Course," aimed at increasing the production of consumer goods and some degree of political relaxation.

The uncertainty, coupled with frustration at the shortages, led to demonstrations. On June 16, 1953, initially because work hours had been increased, construction workers went on strike in East Berlin, close to the central area of Postdamer Platz. The localized demonstrations then spread across the country and caused hundreds of thousands of workers and peasants to take to the streets.[45] The Soviet authorities looked on aghast, the Uprising – in full view of the world (in

---

[43] David Childs and Richard Popplewell, *The Stasi: The East German Intelligence and Security Service* (New York: New York University Press, 1996), p. 52.

[44] Gary Bruce, Resistance with the people: repression and resistance in Eastern Germany, 1945 – 1955 (Oxford: Rowman & Littlefield, 2003), p. 254.

[45] Gregory R. Witkowski, "Peasants Revolt? Re-evaluating the 17 June Uprising in East Germany", *German History*, (24:2, 1 April 2006, pp. 243–266), p. 263, Mary Fulbrook, *History of Germany, 1918-2000: the divided*

Berlin at least) – was a propaganda and public-relations disaster. As a result, the SED government cracked down on the protestors. Thousands were jailed and around 20 (the figure is disputed) were killed as order was restored.[46] Protestors were sentenced to death by firing squad.[47] Stasi detention centers and prisons were now packed. An estimated 13,000 prisoners, 31% of the total prison population, were detained for political reasons by 1956.[48]

The 1953 Uprising had a profound impact on East German society, the SED leadership, and the approach of the MfS. The primary reasons for the crisis were economic mismanagement, political persecution, and the relative increase in living standards seen in West Germany. Therefore, the primary culprit was General Secretary Walter Ulbricht. Nonetheless, Ulbricht managed to outmaneuver other Politburo members who initially attempted to isolate him and emerge from the crisis in more complete control of the SED. In this, he was assisted by Mielke, who helped to depose Zaisser as head of the Stasi. In fact, Zaisser had wanted Ulbricht himself to go.

Ultimately, Zaisser was declared an "enemy of the people" and lived the remainder of his life in isolation. His replacement was Ernst Wollweber, another veteran of the Spanish Civil War who had also gained some credence for his World War II exploits by leading sabotage attempts against the fascist powers.[49] Wollweber began to shift the main functions of the Stasi and to expand its scope. The MfS had failed to read the mood of the population in 1953, and it was a mistake it was determined not to make again. As a result, the active staff in the Ministry expanded into the tens of thousands, and many more resources were put into domestic surveillance and into recruiting more informants. The MfS now sought to understand the sentiments of the DDR, and if necessary its thoughts.[50] As a result, the Stasi took on a distinctly, more sinister flavor after 1953.

---

nation (Oxford: Blackwell, 2002), p. 155.
[46] Mary Fulbrook, *History of Germany, 1918-2000: the divided nation* (Oxford: Blackwell, 2002), p. 155.
[47] Mike Dennis, *The Rise and Fall of the German Democratic Republic 1945-1990* (Harlow: Longman, 2000), p. 68.
[48] Gary Bruce, *Resistance with the people: repression and resistance in Eastern Germany, 1945 – 1955* (Oxford: Rowman & Littlefield, 2003), p. 260.
[49] David Childs and Richard Popplewell, *The Stasi: The East German Intelligence and Security Service* (New York: New York University Press, 1996), p. 54.
[50] Ibid, pp. 60-62.

Wollweber

In some respects, the SED government helped to bring the domestic situation under control after the 1953 Uprising. The notable exception was the huge exodus that accelerated during this period. Unhappy with the lack of economic opportunities and basic goods, as well as the stifling atmosphere created by the Stasi, many East German citizens fled to the West, most through Berlin.

The 1950s was a period of discontent in the so-called Eastern Bloc. A 1956 uprising in Hungary had actually been embraced by the communist government in Budapest, resulting in a Soviet invasion. It would be the first attempt to introduce a variety of "socialism with a human face" (to use the phrase used in Czechoslovakia in 1968). What 1953 and 1956 demonstrated to the citizens of Central and Eastern Europe was that the West would not intervene to support popular movements and anti-communist insurrections. What the Soviets had shown was that they would crush any attempts to move out of its sphere of influence. This created a feeling of resignation amongst the region's inhabitants. As a result, many migrated from the DDR to the West through the "Berlin Corridor," as there were no restrictions on movement around Berlin before 1961.

In addition to political repression, the DDR's economy stagnated in the 1950s. More than a hundred thousand people escaped each year during the decade, and this increased over time. For instance, in 1959, 143,000 East Germans fled to the West and this increased in 1960.[51] From the end of the Second World War until the Berlin Wall was constructed in 1961, an estimated 3.5 million left from East to West Germany.[52] Much of this was caused by economic dissatisfaction. Perhaps the only way Ulbricht and his SED government could have stemmed the flow was through economic reform. Instead, the authorities – for the most part – retained a rigid command economy and tried to influence the population through the security services. The version of the Stasi that lives in the popular imagination began to form during this period, and through the figure of its long term leader, Erich Mielke.

Erich Mielke and Markus Wolf

Wollweber was in charge of the MfS for four years until he was the victim of another Ulbricht-Mielke purge. Years later, it was reported that Mielke had briefed Ulbricht that Wollweber was an alcoholic.[53] Whatever the real reason, Mielke wasted no time in stamping his authority on the Stasi when he was appointed at the end of 1957. He was to lead the organization for 41 years, until the death throes of the DDR itself.

Mielke was born in Berlin in 1907. A lifelong communist, he had committed assassinations (in the name of the KPD) during the 1930s, when Germany was still governed by the Weimar Republic. He fought in the Spanish Civil War and subsequently worked as a Soviet spy. After exile during the Second World War, he returned to the Soviet zone in Germany after the end of the conflict to help forge the new communist republic.

Above all, Mielke helped the DDR develop its peculiar security setup. The expansion of the scope and importance of the Stasi in maintaining SED dominance over East Germany was crucial. Mielke was the consummate Apparatchik (communist party official and insider).[54] He understood how the state and its bureaucracy functioned and exploited this to the full. Mielke

---

[51] Gary Bruce, *Resistance with the people: repression and resistance in Eastern Germany, 1945 – 1955* (Oxford: Rowman & Littlefield, 2003), p. 261.
[52] Mary Fulbrook, *History of Germany, 1918-2000: the divided nation* (Oxford: Blackwell, 2002), p. 158.
[53] David Childs and Richard Popplewell, *The Stasi: The East German Intelligence and Security Service* (New York: New York University Press, 1996), p. 65.
[54] Ibid.

also had a specific method that he applied to the MfS and its practices.

Under Mielke, the security services moved from using overt physical threat and violence to a more subtle and total surveillance.[55] Mielke's Stasi was the true manifestation of the Orwellian state, Big Brother. Firstly, Mielke vastly increased the number of full-time employees at the MfS, which tripled between 1957 and 1973 from 17,500-52,700.[56] Secondly, the MfS expanded its surveillance activities with this new staff, opening files and identifying suspects across East German society. Thirdly, it began to incorporate unofficial operatives or informants, known as Inoffizielle Mitarbeiter, or IM.[57] These informants were either enthusiastic party members, sympathetic to the regime's objectives, or coerced into cooperation. The Stasi under Mielke preyed on human weakness, using embarrassing or scandalous personal behavior as a recruiting tactic. Reasons could include alcohol consumption or extramarital affairs.[58] Prostitutes were used as informants, and the trail would lead on from the threat of the resulting humiliation.[59] Family members, in true Orwellian fashion, were encouraged to spy on each other.[60] The result was a general climate of suspicion and fear amongst the general population. The Stasi was driven by the need for total control, and to prevent the events of 1953 from happening again. Spies even informed on one another.[61]

Spying in the DDR was not restricted to the domestic sphere. The security apparatus included a much smaller foreign intelligence unit, the infamous Hauptverwaltung Aufklärung (HVA), or main department of reconnaissance. The HVA was led by Markus Wolf, who developed a somewhat legendary reputation as a master spy.[62] Such was Wolf's notoriety that it is believed he inspired the character of Karla, the communist intelligence boss in John Le Carré's Cold War novels *Tinker Tailor Soldier Spy* and *The Spy Who Came in From the Cold*.[63] Historians have cast doubt over how expert Wolf really, was but the HVA certainly delivered outcomes that were embarrassing for the West, and with only a relatively small number of full-time employees (about 4,000).[64] Wolf headed the HVA for 34 years, from 1952 until his retirement in 1986.[65]

---

[55] Mary Fulbrook, *History of Germany, 1918-2000: the divided nation* (Oxford: Blackwell, 2002), p. 204, Uwe Spiekermann (ed), 'The Stasi at Home and Abroad: Domestic Order and Foreign Intelligence', *Bulletin of the German Historical Institute*, 9 (2014), pp. 14-15.
[56] Mike Dennis, *The Rise and Fall of the German Democratic Republic 1945-1990* (Harlow: Longman, 2000), p. 103.
[57] Mary Fulbrook, *History of Germany, 1918-2000: the divided nation* (Oxford: Blackwell, 2002), p. 212.
[58] Mike Dennis, *The Rise and Fall of the German Democratic Republic 1945-1990* (Harlow: Longman, 2000), p. 222.
[59] Ibid, p. 153.
[60] Ibid, p. 152.
[61] Ibid, p. 103.
[62] David Childs and Richard Popplewell, *The Stasi: The East German Intelligence and Security Service* (New York: New York University Press, 1996), p. 113.
[63] Mike Dennis, *The Rise and Fall of the German Democratic Republic 1945-1990* (Harlow: Longman, 2000), p. 223.
[64] David Childs and Richard Popplewell, *The Stasi: The East German Intelligence and Security Service* (New York: New York University Press, 1996), p. 112.
[65] Uwe Spiekermann (ed), 'The Stasi at Home and Abroad: Domestic Order and Foreign Intelligence', *Bulletin of*

Wolf

Strengthening the KGB

There was no major change in the KGB until 1967, apart from minor structural changes in the fall of 1966, when the Accounting and Archival Division became the Tenth Division. The group under the KGB Chairman for the study and generalization of the work experience of state security bodies was transformed into a group of assistants, and the Eleventh Division, responsible for coordinating communications with state security organs of the socialist countries, was created. As an independent unit, it did not last long.

Despite frequent changes of KGB chairmen, the state security agencies survived the crisis provoked by the personnel and structural reforms of the mid-1950s. With that, the KGB became more active in the roles of protecting state and military secrets. On October 1, 1965, a new "instruction to ensure the safety of state secrets and the regime of secrecy of ongoing work" was approved.

On May 18, 1967, Yuri Andropov was named the new Secretary of the CPSU Central Committee. He remained in this post for 15 years, longer than any other colleague in Soviet times, and he immensely boosted the KGB's reputation, despite the fact he would be blamed by the public for the Soviets' costly fighting in Afghanistan in the 1980s. The Fifth Department of the KGB was created by Andropov to organize counter-intelligence work and combat the ideological sabotage in the country. In fact, any important appointment could only take place with the approval of the State Security Committee in all spheres, from the ministry to industry, from art to sports.

Andropov

At the same time, there was an improvement in operational search activities. For example, in 1964, the "instruction on the procedure for carrying out operational and technical measures in the practice of the operative-intelligence and investigation work of the KGB" was adopted. In particular, this allowed the use of "Providence," complex operational measures, to confirm the connection of GRU officer Oleg Penkovsky with British and US intelligence services.

"Operation 100," a plan of agent and operational activities, had been developed to increase the level of counter-intelligence work among foreigners in 1965. Initially, it covered the European part of the country and the Caucasus, but eventually it spread to Central Asia. The purpose of this plan was to coordinate the actions of counter-intelligence units on a national scale.

Based on the experience of "Operation 100," a prospective counterintelligence work plan was developed in 1967 called "Operation Horizon." That year, amongst foreigners who had come to the USSR for a short time, more than 250 officers and agents of special services of foreign states were identified. Over 100 of them were convicted and expelled from the USSR.

There was much progress in the fight against corruption. Andropov's subordinates earned huge wages for the time, but they were strongly punished in cases of corruption. Also under his leadership, special detachments "Alpha" and "Vympel" were created to destroy terrorists and release hostages.

In accordance with the tasks set by the June (1967) Plenum of the Central Committee of the CPSU, the main focus of the KGB was above all else to strengthen foreign policy, to contribute to the successful implementation of Soviet foreign policy to ensure timely identification, and the exposure of the subversive plans of imperialist states and their intelligence agencies. One of the first steps in this direction was the strengthening of the intelligence service by experienced Chekists, both in the central apparatus and abroad.

Following the instructions of the CPSU Central Committee, the KGB carried out a series of measures to strengthen the fight against the anti-Soviet activities of Chinese opponents of Communism and ensure the reliable protection of the Soviet border with China. The KGB worked to establish several intelligence units in the territories and regions bordering China.

Giving high priority to the timely receipt of secret information about the subversive intentions of the enemies, the KGB intelligence service took steps to enhance their agents' positions, primarily in the U.S. Strengthening the intelligence apparatus of the intelligence service helped to obtain important information on political, military, scientific, and technical problems. The main attention in the matter of increasing the level of counter-intelligence work in the country was focused on further improvements to countering military, economic, and political espionage.

Thanks to this work, the KGB would successfully identify many operations carried out by enemy intelligence services in certain areas of the Soviet Union, particularly the Far East, the Baltic countries, and the border regions of the Ukraine. The counter-intelligence service carried out operations resulting in the photographing of 54 documents of ambassadors to NATO member countries, annual reports of some military attaches to other embassies, classified materials on political, military-economic, operational, and other issues.

Measures to identify and suppress the hostile activities of anti-Soviet elements among churchmen and sectarians were also undertaken, taking into account the ideologically harmful activities of religious and Zionist centers. 122 KGB agents were sent abroad to reveal their intentions, to disrupt the subversive actions they had prepared, and to carry out other counter-intelligence assignments.

At the same time, it was possible to attribute criminal liability for illegal activities to a number of active sectarians. According to official KGB reports in 1975, the main efforts were focused on "improving measures to effectively counter the enemy's intelligence aspirations, reliable protection of state and military secrets, and suppression of hostile ideological sabotage."

On July 5, 1978, the KGB under the USSR Council of Ministers was renamed the USSR State Security Committee, but the system and structure of the KGB bodies remained unchanged. The second half of the 1970s and the beginning of the 1980s did not differ significantly from the previous period, and Andropov was still the chairman of the KGB.

In 1978, foreign intelligence received documents and other valuable materials regarding the foreign and domestic policies of the United States and China, as well as their subversive activities against the USSR and the Warsaw Bloc countries. The activities of the governing bodies of NATO were also covered.

As this all makes clear, at the height of the Cold War, the KGB focused its attention not on the repression of USSR dissidents, but on countering the activities of foreign special services. That said, Andropov also actively opposed the emergence of nationalist and church-sectarian organizations. The head of the KGB named certain representatives of the Catholic, Jewish, and Muslim clergy, as well as leaders of such sects as Baptists, Seventh Day Adventists, Jehovah's Witnesses, and Pentecostals, as the main ideological opponents. In this regard, the attention of the fifth KGB units was directed to the timely suppression of the activities of the emissaries of the foreign missions of these sects. There were many other religious organizations whose activities were prohibited in the Soviet Union, such as "Underground Evangelism" (USA), "Light in the East" (FRG), "Institute for the Study of Religion and Communism" (England), "Friedenstimme" (FRG), "Foreign Mission of the Council of Churches of the European Baptist Church" (USA), etc.

Special attention was paid by Andropov to Zionism, considering the Soviet Union had mostly allied with the Arab world as the West supported Israel. In his opinion, the enemies of the USSR actively used Zionism and specific pro-Zionist elements for subversive purposes.

High Socialism and Supreme Control

Emigration was becoming an increasing problem by the start of the 1960s, not only for the DDR but for Moscow, which recognized the exodus undermined the socialist system and its geopolitical bloc. In addition, the Kremlin resented Western influence in East Germany. The migration was driven primarily by economic opportunities and by this point the BRD had raced ahead of its eastern counterparts. It was obvious that if citizens wanted a materially better quality of life, it was in their best interests to move to the West. Then there was the increasingly stifling atmosphere in the DDR, caused by the Stasi.

The situation reached a crisis point in August 1961. Already in that year, 160,000 Easterners had registered in West Berlin.[66] Earlier that year American President John F. Kennedy, freshly inaugurated, had met his Soviet counterpart Nikita Khrushchev in Vienna. The Soviet leader had believed he had the measure of an inexperienced politician and sought to exploit what he saw as weakness. This approach was to bring victories, as in Berlin, and then a nearly massive miscalculation during the Cuban Missile Crisis the following year.

On the evening of August 12, 1961, 40,000 DDR soldiers (observed by two Soviet divisions, which stayed outside the city) sealed the borders between East and West Berlin, initially using crude barbed wire. This was to become known in the West as the Berlin Wall, or Berliner Mauer to West Germans. To DDR citizens, now cut adrift from their brethren in the West, it was officially the "Anti-Fascist Protective Rampart." It would remain in place for 28 years until its fall in November 1989.

There were numerous escape attempts, some through ingenious means such as hiding in car engines or swimming across the bottom of the River Spree.[67] The simple alternative was the so-called "Death Strip" between the two Berlins, but as the name suggested, that was not advisable.[68] The East German security services were now in charge of policing this internal border.

Indeed, the Stasi had already been active in border security before 1961. 16 people had been killed trying to cross the inner-Berlin border, while 100 had been killed along the DDR-BRD demarcation line.[69] The MfS was assisted in this task by the VoPo or Volkspolizei (People's Police), and the number of those killed would drastically increase after 1961.

After 1961 the SED believed it had achieved control of the country by sealing its borders. Paradoxically, there was a minor thaw in the oppressiveness of the regime as Ulbricht and his Politburo sought to build a specifically East German socialism. Nevertheless, it required continued Stasi vigilance, and the Stasi would develop even more sophisticated operations in the 1960s.

---

[66] Gary Bruce, *Resistance with the people: repression and resistance in Eastern Germany, 1945 – 1955* (Oxford: Rowman & Littlefield, 2003), p. 261.
[67] Mary Fulbrook, *History of Germany, 1918-2000: the divided nation* (Oxford: Blackwell, 2002), p. 264.
[68] Konrad H. Jarausch and Helga A. Welsh, "Two Germanies, 1961-1989", German History in Documents and Images (German Historical Institute: http://germanhistorydocs.ghi-dc.org/, [accessed 6 October 2017], p. 2.
[69] Mike Dennis, *The Rise and Fall of the German Democratic Republic 1945-1990* (Harlow: Longman, 2000), p. 100.

There were only a few moments in the history of the DDR when the country appeared to have an outward appearance of calm. In the 1960s, although the state was not recognized by many countries due to the BRD's "Hallstein Doctrine," the SED began to build its version of East German socialism, and the Stasi played a key role in this development. As its techniques evolved, the Stasi moved from physical violence to a system of social engineering.[70] The climate it fostered within the DDR imposed a degree of uniformity on the population by incentivizing expected or acceptable behaviors.

By the 1960s, the MfS had started monitoring DDR citizens' communications. Up to 3000 Stasi employees looked through postal correspondence as well as telephone calls. Opened post was labelled, incredibly, as "damaged in transit."[71] It became a feature of life in East Germany. In addition, teams of Stasi agents put listening devices in the flats and houses of those, for whatever reason, under suspicion. The intruders would notoriously leave subtle signs that they had been there, designed to intimidate the resident. This is fictionalized in the 2006 film by director Florian Henckel von Donnersmarck's *The Lives of Others* (German: *Das Leben der Anderen*).

Nevertheless, Stasi oppression could be relaxed somewhat by the introduction, surprisingly by Ulbricht, of the Neues Ökonomisches System (New Economic System) in the mid-1960s.[72] State-owned enterprises began to produce "luxury" goods such as the Trabant car (known as "Trabi" to Germans), even though waiting lists proved to be long. Ulbricht's Neues Ökonomisches System allowed minor economic liberalization. This in turn led to some political freedoms, including greater access to music and literature.[73] The New Economic System, however, proved relatively short-lived because many in the SED high command resented the very limited liberalisations and were hostile as a result.[74] The DDR, however, did not experience the student unrest that occurred in Western societies during the 1960s (as well as non-Western ones such as Czechoslovakia and Yugoslavia), most notably the BRD. Put simply, the threat of jail managed to deter would-be student activists.[75] In fact, the Stasi and its associated departments were faced with a new challenge at the end of the 1960s because there were dissidents from the BRD who were actually sympathetic to their socialist regime.

Part of the DDR security apparatus sought to undermine the stability of the BRD and its

---

[70] Uwe Spiekermann (ed), 'The Stasi at Home and Abroad: Domestic Order and Foreign Intelligence', *Bulletin of the German Historical Institute*, 9 (2014), p. 15.
[71] Anna Funder, *Stasiland: Stories From Behind the Berlin Wall* (London: Granta, 2003), quoted in Rachel Clark, ''Everything about everyone': the depth of Stasi surveillance in the GDR', *The View East*, 23 July 2009, https://thevieweast.wordpress.com/tag/stasi/, [accessed 10 January 2018]
[72] Ibid, p. 164.
[73] Andrew Evans, "The Last Gasp of Socialism: Economics and Culture in 1960s East Germany", *German Life and Letters*, (63, 2010, pp. 331–344), p. 332, Mary Fulbrook, *History of Germany, 1918-2000: the divided nation* (Oxford: Blackwell, 2002), pp. 164-165.
[74] Mary Fulbrook, *History of Germany, 1918-2000: the divided nation* (Oxford: Blackwell, 2002), p. 166.
[75] Doris M. Epler, *The Berlin Wall: How it Rose and Why it Fell* (Brookfield: The Millbrook Press, 1992), p. 82.

Western allies. It was, therefore, presented with a gift via the advent of the Rote Armee Fraktion (Red Army Faction, or RAF). The RAF formed in the wake of demonstrations held in 1968, opposing the ambivalent position of the BRD government towards many issues of the day. Protests against the Shah of Iran's visit to West Berlin in 1967, and against the Vietnam War in Frankfurt in 1968, prompted heavy-handed police action. This subsequently motivated communists and other left-wingers to organize against a state they considered to be still governed by ex-Nazis. Their issues ranged from Western military intervention to anti-imperialism and anti-capitalism. A number of these, led by journalist Ulrike Meinhof and renegade Andreas Baader, formed the RAF in 1970. The group then launched numerous acts of sabotage, kidnappings, and other kinds of violence.

After the original leaders were arrested, subsequent "generations" of the RAF were spawned. This presented a challenge to the Stasi, in particular its foreign intelligence arm, the HVA. The activities of the RAF provided the HVA with an opportunity to infiltrate West German society. This was hardly new, and the department had achieved numerous successes to this end from the 1950s and as a result, repeatedly embarrassed the BRD authorities.[76] The RAF, however, was different. Whereas the normal practice of the HVA was to infiltrate public and government institutions to derive intelligence, the RAF was a more combustible proposition. The HVA had to be careful not to appear to be stoking violent acts in West German territory or actively encouraging insurrection. In addition, the HVA was deeply suspicious of the RAF and its motives.[77] Its members may have been self-professed communists (which was more than could be said for many East Germans, who essentially had no choice), but they were unpredictable, violent, and from the West. In fact, the HVA and SED were embarrassed when it was reported that wanted-RAF terrorists were being harbored in the DDR.

All told, it is difficult to gauge the extent of the links between the HVA and RAF, which certainly would have been ultra-top-secret. It may be that = Wolf and his staff kept its distance from the West German revolutionaries, hoping to keep the group in reserve as a means of destabilizing the West as and when it needed them.[78] In any case, the RAF still functioned and carried out various actions until well into the 1990s. The legacy of this left-wing guerilla group, and the BRD's response to it, still resonates today.[79]

The Guillaume Scandal

The late 1960s saw another change in the relationship between West Germany and East Germany. The rise to power in the BRD of Willy Brandt caused a change in policy direction that

---

[76] David Childs and Richard Popplewell, *The Stasi: The East German Intelligence and Security Service* (New York: New York University Press, 1996), p. 143.
[77] Ibid, p. 141.
[78] Ibid, p. 141.
[79] Deutsche Welle, 'The legacy of the 1977 German Autumn of left-wing terror', 5 September 2017, http://www.dw.com/en/the-legacy-of-the-1977-german-autumn-of-left-wing-terror/a-40365602 [accessed 17 January 2018]

advocated conciliation with the communist bloc, including the DDR. Brandt would be the leading figure of what the West Germans dubbed Ostpolitik. For the SED, it struggled to exist in the international arena due to lack of recognition. This was part of the BRD's stated "Hallstein Doctrine" (named after the Foreign Ministry official who authored the policy), whereby the Federal Republic of Germany would not do business with any country that recognized the DDR.[80] Brandt, however, executed a complete reversal in East-West relations by attempting to build a dialogue with the BRD's neighbors. He met with DDR Prime Minister Willi Stoph in March 1970, visited Poland with a remarkable demonstration of contrition over Germany's wartime crimes, and subsequently signed treaties with Moscow and Warsaw later that year.[81] Brandt signed the "Basic Treaty" in 1972 that appeared to accept the existence of the DDR – although not categorically – and thereby satisfied one of the SED's cherished aims.

Stoph

The benefits for the DDR were clear. The state was admitted to the UN and finally achieved some degree of legitimacy. It managed to acquire desperately needed hard currency, reduced its indebtedness and led to an increase in trade.[82] What Brandt and Bonn achieved through Ostpolitik was not immediately obvious, but the strategy paid dividends over time and has been identified as a key reason the Berlin Wall eventually fell. There were political casualties,

---

[80] William Glenn Gray, *Germany's Cold War: The Global Campaign to Isolate East Germany, 1949-1969* (London: University of North Carolina Press, 2003), p. 223.
[81] Ibid.
[82] M.E. Sarotte, *Dealing with the Devil: East Germany, Detente, and Ostpolitik, 1969-1973,* (The University of North Carolina Press, 2001), p. 164.

however, on both sides. Brandt and Ulbricht were deemed weak by their respective hardliners and, as a result, made enemies.[83] In addition, the U.S. – particularly National Security Advisor and Secretary of State Henry Kissinger – was concerned Ostpolitik would cause a resurgence in German nationalism.[84] DDR leader Walter Ulbricht was removed from office in 1971 by pro-Moscow hawks in the Politburo. Curiously, his successor, Erich Honecker, then appeared to pursue an identical strategy.[85]

Ulbricht, who had been leader of the DDR for over 20 years, met the fate of so many communist politicians once deposed - the Stasi monitored and spied on Ulbricht until his death in 1973.[86] Willy Brandt's political demise, however, came as a direct result of the work of the Stasi and caused an international sensation.

There was limited access for Westerners into East Germany. Those who did enter the country were often treated with deep suspicion and monitored.[87] The same was not true when East Germans came to the BRD. The West Germans actively encouraged East Germans to defect and even gave them welcome money, Begrüßungsgeld. Therefore, it is perhaps surprising that the DDR security services exploited this for both information and political sabotage. The most significant of the many East German spies exposed in the BRD during the Cold War was Günter Guillaume, the Willy Brandt adviser who was revealed to be a Stasi agent, triggering the West German Chancellor's resignation.

Guillaume was born in Berlin and had been a Nazi Party member during the Second World War. He was then recruited by the Stasi during the 1950s and instructed to move to the BRD in 1956 to work his way up the ladder of the Social Democratic Party (SPD), West Germany's mainstream center-left political party. The Stasi could not have anticipated how well this mission would work out.[88]

In 1972, Guillaume became a close adviser to the Federal Republic's SPD Chancellor, Willy Brandt. He was then able to transmit intelligence back to his political masters in Berlin. The West German intelligence agencies, however, began to suspect Guillaume of feeding information back to the HVA, and to Markus Wolf. It is believed the West Germans were tipped off by the French authorities after testimony from a Soviet defector in 1973.[89]

---

[83] Ibid, p. 164.
[84] Niall Ferguson, *Kissinger 1923-1968: The Idealist* (London: Allen Lane, 2015), p. 703.
[85] M.E. Sarotte, *Dealing with the Devil : East Germany, Detente, and Ostpolitik, 1969-1973*, (The University of North Carolina Press, 2001), p. 168
[86] Mike Dennis, *The Rise and Fall of the German Democratic Republic 1945-1990* (Harlow: Longman, 2000), p. 138.
[87] Godfrey Hodgson, *People's Century: From the Dawn of the Century to the Eve of the Millennium* (BBC Books, 1998), p. 582.
[88] David Childs and Richard Popplewell, *The Stasi: The East German Intelligence and Security Service* (New York: New York University Press, 1996), p. 112.
[89] Patrick Pesnot, Great Spies of the 20th Century, (Barnsley: Pen & Sword Military, 2016), p. 137.

In April 1974, Guillaume was arrested by police, and in the ensuing scandal, the unwitting Willy Brandt was forced to resign. Guillaume was charged with treason and imprisoned but released back to the DDR in 1981 as part of a prisoner exchange. He was given a hero's welcome upon his return. Brandt believed that Wolf had intended to oust him through the Guillaume affair, a charge Wolf refuted; Wolf had, after all, lost his direct link to the BRD Chancellor. In addition, Brandt was replaced by Helmut Schmidt, who was more hawkish towards the communist bloc and later supported the deployment of American Pershing nuclear missiles into BRD territory.

Guillaume and Brandt (left)

Another development emerged involving the Stasi during the early 1970s which could have been much more dangerous had details come out at the time. Though few were aware, the Stasi was assisting a number of terrorist groups, [90] and one of the most damaging was its links to the terrorists who committed the attack on Israeli athletes during the 1972 Munich Olympic Games. A Palestinian terrorist group, Black September, broke into the Olympic village and took the 11 Israeli athletes hostage, and after a bungled attempt to negotiate with the terrorists, followed by a bungled rescue mission, all the Israeli hostages were killed.

The world reacted with outrage, but this was an era of international terrorism, hostage taking and plane hijacking. There were an almost countless number of groups across the world with various grievances and causes, and among the most common were left-wing and nationalist organisations. As it turned out, the Stasi had offered assistance to many of them.

After the 1972 atrocity, the East German government offered support to Black September and

---

[90] Mary Fulbrook, *History of Germany, 1918-2000: the divided nation* (Oxford: Blackwell, 2002), p. 230.

the Palestinian Liberation Organisation (PLO).[91] East German intelligence was also implicated in the downing of a Convair Flight 330 in Switzerland, which was on its way to Tel Aviv in February 1970. The same day, a bomb exploded on an Austrian Airlines flight shortly after taking off from Frankfurt am Main.[92] It is believed that the Stasi also provided assistance to terrorist groups such as the Irish Republic Army (IRA) in its conflict against the British, as well as the ETA (Basque Homeland and Liberty) in its armed rebellion in Spain.[93] The DDR also provided a refuge for RAF terrorists and other "fellow travelers" who had anti-capitalist and anti-Western sympathies. This strategy was consistent with the Stasi's objective of destabilizing the West wherever and whenever possible.

The DDR did not only focus its foreign policy within Europe. From the 1960s, the SED attempted to improve relations with the postcolonial and non-aligned world.[94] This involved supporting liberation movements in the decolonized world and visiting leaders, such as Gamal Abdul Nasser, in Egypt.[95] This became known as Afrikapolitik.

The SED under both Ulbricht and Honecker was desperate for legitimacy,[96] and Afrikapolitik was a manifestation of this need. In addition, the DDR sought hard currency and access to raw materials. Honecker expanded the policy by visiting Libya, Angola, Mozambique, Tanzania and Ethiopia.[97]

While the political leadership provided the diplomatic side of Afrikapolitik, the Stasi, in particular the HVA, provided undercover and military assistance. For instance, weapons and hardware were supplied to militant groups such as the African National Congress in South Africa, to the Zimbabwe African National Union (ZANU) and South West Africa People's Organization (SWAPO) in Namibia.[98]

The Stasi and Daily Life

By the 1970s, the Stasi had almost achieved complete operational surveillance in the domestic sphere. This was known as flächendeckenden Überwachung (comprehensive surveillance).[99] It

---

[91] Jeffrey Herf, 'East Germany's Assault on Israel', *Commentary Magazine*, 16 May 2016, https://www.commentarymagazine.com/articles/east-germanys-assault-israel/, [accessed 11 January 2018]

[92] John R. Schindler, 'This Mass Murder Mystery Has Terrorism, Spies, Palestinians, Stasi and the FBI', *Observer*, 16 September 2016, http://observer.com/2016/09/this-mass-murder-mystery-has-terrorism-spies-palestinians-stasi-and-the-fbi/, [accessed 11 January 2018]

[93] Mike Dennis, *The Rise and Fall of the German Democratic Republic 1945-1990* (Harlow: Longman, 2000), p. 217.

[94] Gareth M. Winrow, *The Foreign Policy of the GDR in Africa* (Cambridge: Cambridge University Press, 1990)

[95] Ibid, p. 113.

[96] Ibid, p. 221.

[97] Ibid, p. 113.

[98] Deutsche Welle, "Africa and communist East Germany", [accessed 18 October 2017], http://www.dw.com/en/africa-and-communist-east-germany/g-18753769

[99] Rainer Eckert, 'Flächendeckender Überwachung', *Der Spiegel*, 1 January 1993, http://www.spiegel.de/spiegel/spiegelspecial/d-55475506.html, [accessed 12 January 2018]

was not only average citizens who were being monitored and spied upon, as the Stasi managed to incorporate artists, writers and the cultural intelligentsia into its web.[100] A number of the DDR's best known artists collaborated with the Stasi, including Christa Wolf, Sascha Anderson, Ibrahim Böhme and Wolfgang Schnur.[101] Christa Wolf was a writer whose best known book was probably *Kassandra*, and she was often outwardly critical of the SED regime. Taken together, this can be seen as part of the totalitarian state. After the fall of the DDR, so-called collaborators such as Wolf were vilified by the unified German press. This however, was a misunderstanding of the constricting nature of East German society and the reach of the MfS's tentacles.

One of the few places that avoided this influence was the church. An unlikely source of resistance against both the SED regime and its Stasi security forces, churches have been described as offering the opportunity for "muted dissent."[102] Poland, despite the communist government, maintained a strong commitment to Catholicism during the Cold War, and the visits of Polish Pope John Paul II have been cited as a key ingredient in weakening communist rule in the country. Less has been written about the DDR in this respect, probably because church meetings were more covert, at least until the Leipzig marches at the end of the 1980s.

How impermeable, however, were the churches from the prying eyes of the Stasi? The DDR was unusual for a communist country insofar as it was majority Protestant, rather than a Catholic or Orthodox Christian country. The church certainly became a focal point for unhappiness within the regime and other prohibited activities, such as a cover for gay and lesbian groups from the early 1980s.[103] In fact the church had, taken together, a moderate vision for reform of the communist system, a variant of Czechoslovak leader Alexander Dubček's "socialism with a human face" and Gorbachev's "Glasnost."

Inevitably though, it is wishful thinking to suggest that the Stasi did not infiltrate the church. There is evidence to suggest that there were numerous informants within religious groups.[104]

Naturally, the Stasi also impacted other cultural aspects of life in East Germany. Erich Mielke, head of the Stasi for most of the DDR's existence, was a keen sports fan, especially football. As a result, sport came to represent another bizarre and cynical chapter in the history of the Stasi. Mielke was a staunch supporter of the Dynamo Berlin football club and was the club's chairman. It may have been a coincidence, but Dynamo won the East German football league every season between 1979 and 1988.[105] It was later reported that the Stasi "owned" FC Dynamo Berlin.

---

[100] Mike Dennis, *The Rise and Fall of the German Democratic Republic 1945-1990* (Harlow: Longman, 2000), p. 146.
[101] Ibid, p. 221.
[102] Mary Fulbrook, *History of Germany, 1918-2000: the divided nation* (Oxford: Blackwell, 2002), p. 59.
[103] German Historical Institute, 'Homosexuality in East Germany', *Two Germanies*, http://germanhistorydocs.ghi-dc.org/sub_document.cfm?document_id=1108, [accessed 12 January 2018]
[104] Mary Fulbrook, *History of Germany, 1918-2000: the divided nation* (Oxford: Blackwell, 2002), pp. 242-243.
[105] Mike Dennis, *The Rise and Fall of the German Democratic Republic 1945-1990* (Harlow: Longman, 2000), p. 208.

Hanns Leske, a historian of football in the DDR, said that the club was "frowned on by football supporters and hated by the East German public." It appears that the Stasi was intent on extinguishing any dissent in both the political and football arenas.[106]

As part of its recognition and legitimacy strategy, the DDR, led by the Stasi, sought international sporting success. The most notable part of this approach was the Olympic doping program. From the late 1960s, athletes in East Germany were given a variety of hormones, steroids, and performance-enhancing drugs. The MfS was able to effectively quarantine the competitors and only allow them to take part in overseas events when the athletes would pass doping tests. Many of the athletes were unaware that they were being used as guinea pigs, and in later years many had long-term health problems.[107] When they were abroad, DDR competitors were accompanied by Stasi agents.[108]

The results achieved thanks to these dubious tactics were spectacular. East Germany won 20 gold medals at the 1972 Munich Olympic Games, 40 in Montreal during 1976, and 47 in Moscow during 1980. Even in 1988, when the wider world was already very suspicious of the DDR's tactics, the East German team won 37 gold medals. Remarkably, the DDR's Olympic team finished consistently second in the final medals table.

The story of sports inside and outside the DDR is indicative of life in the country overall. The Stasi played a major role in corrupting sports, which should otherwise have been a source of relief from the everyday grind of life in a communist state. That the Stasi attempted (and succeeded) in cheating to further its own aims demonstrates the utter moral bankruptcy of the SED and the MfS.

Elimination

By the beginning of the 1980s, the Soviet Union seriously lagged behind the advanced Western countries. The civilian branches of the economy developed extremely slowly, with billions of rubles spent on the arms race and the maintenance of the army. The outdated political system also hampered the development of the country.

In 1985, the Soviet Union was headed by Mikhail Gorbachev, an energetic leader who announced the beginning of perestroika, intended to accelerate economic growth by absorbing new technologies and by strengthening discipline and people's interest in the results of their work. In foreign policy, Gorbachev expressed his support for a new course, which he labeled

---

[106] David Crossland, 'Dynamo Berlin: The soccer club 'owned' by the Stasi', *CNN*, 14 January 2016, http://edition.cnn.com/2016/01/13/football/dynamo-berlin-stasi-east-germany-football/index.html, [accessed 12 January 2018]

[107] William Glenn Gray, *Germany's Cold War: The Global Campaign to Isolate East Germany, 1949-1969* (London: University of North Carolina Press, 2003), p. 220.

[108] Mike Dennis, *The Rise and Fall of the German Democratic Republic 1945-1990* (Harlow: Longman, 2000), p. 208.

"new thinking." The USSR became less confrontational with the West, and negotiations were held with President Reagan. During these meetings, agreements were reached on the relaxation of international tension and the reduction of nuclear stockpiles.

Gorbachev

Gorbachev and Reagan

Throughout this time, the KGB still worried that the United States and NATO countries sought to achieve a major strategic advantage over the Soviet Union, and the deplorable economic situation of the Soviet Union greatly hampered its competition with the West. In early 1985, the KGB reported the danger of the "subversive actions" of the West, which it claimed aimed to cause "serious economic damage" to the Soviet bloc. Immediate danger came where Soviet grain imports were concerned. According to a KGB report, "Using some difficulties in the production of agricultural products in our country, the United States is trying to put the USSR in dependence on grain imports, aiming to use this food weapon in the future to exert pressure on the Soviet Union." (Sever, 2008). While the West believed that the Soviet Union was receiving grain and other food at low prices, the KGB considered it exploitation.

The KGB also worried that without changes in the composition of Soviet leadership, Soviet economic problems would continue, which meant that Western countries would try to take advantage and exploit them. Refusing to consider that the problem lay in the Soviet system itself, the KGB expected Gorbachev to make it dynamic, bringing the necessary discipline to overcome the Soviet Union's economic stagnation and establish a reliable "balance of power" with the West. The KGB carefully instructed Gorbachev on all issues, hoping he could make a great impression on the Politburo with his knowledge of both Soviet and international problems.

During Gorbachev's time, the KGB numbered up to 400,000 employees in the Soviet Union, 200,000 border troops, and an extensive network of freelancers, but external intelligence remained the most prestigious division of the KGB. Except for the modest expansion of the states in the Pacific region and in several new consulates in other regions, the KGB did not increase its presence abroad at the beginning of the Gorbachev era. Moreover, the fall in oil prices and the aggravated economic crisis in the USSR reduced the inflow of currency the KGB needed to expand its activities.

As the Warsaw Treaty Organization disintegrated, the Kremlin withdrew hundreds of thousands of its soldiers from Eastern Europe and the ideological foundation of the Soviet state collapsed. As a result, the prestige of Moscow as the center of Communism fell. The crisis of the Soviet economy inevitably led to the reduction of aid to developing countries, and consequently, the role of intelligence became increasingly important as a means of preserving the influence of the Soviet Union both inside and outside its borders.

One of the main functions of Soviet foreign intelligence according to Gorbachev was scientific and technical espionage. The collection of scientific and technical information in the most important area—defense—was coordinated in the early 1980s by the Military Industrial Commission (MIC), which, under Gorbachev, received the status of the State Commission for its Military-Industrial Complex. Perhaps the greatest success of the Military-Industrial Complex was the copying of the American Air Warning and Control System (AWACS) and the B-1B bomber (which became the Soviet bomber "Blackjack").

In the summer of 1988, Gorbachev warmly responded to the "purposeful work" of the leadership of the KGB, "aimed at improving activities in conditions created by a new stage in the development of democratic processes."

In early 1989, Vladimir Kryuchkov became the first chairman in the history of the KGB to meet the U.S. ambassador while in office. In the following months, he and other senior KGB officers gave interviews and press conferences to Western correspondents, even appearing in the movie *KGB Today*, which was offered to foreign television companies (Mlechin, 2017).

Convinced that Gorbachev was leading the process to destroy the Soviet system in August 1991, Kryuchkov became one of the leaders of the coup against Gorbachev. For a time, Gorbachev was essentially under house arrest, but the coup ultimately failed and resulted in the of Kryuchkov and other conspirators.

As the Soviet Union headed towards its collapse in the early 1990s and the Red Curtain began to fall, the KGB made every effort to deny its violent past and predecessors. However, the Russian people, as they learned more and more details of the KGB's terrible history, inevitably wondered if it were possible to rebuild such an organization at all. And naturally, as Soviet influence diminished in Eastern Europe, locals who had suffered repression for decades condemned security services like the KGB.

From the beginning of the October Revolution, the Communist leaders had felt the need for both internal security agencies and intelligence, but in the 1990s, Russia quickly learned it was necessary for its agencies to have the trust and respect of its citizens. With that, it was necessary to close the KGB and start over again. The process of formally terminating the KGB began in August 1991 and came to a close in January 1992.

The End of the Stasi

As the DDR entered its final decade, the so-called "Stasi State" was fully formed. The number of official Stasi agents, as well as informants - IM (*inoffizielle Mitarbeiter*) - had reached epic proportions. The Stasi had penetrated every sphere of society, even family and personal life. Many East German inhabitants had been browbeaten into conformity, knowing what to say, when to say it, and to whom. The same was true across the communist bloc, including in the Soviet Union, but the extent of Stasi spying and the scope of its control was particularly unique even amongst its peers in Central and Eastern Europe.

As with all dictatorships built on fear rather than consent, the DDR was outwardly stable but inwardly brittle. The Stasi was hated by East Germans, and the regime was ridiculed by DDR citizens in private. Crucially, the Stasi – and the SED regime more generally - was utterly corrupt, which meant East Germans could not rely upon an objective rule of law. They knew that certain rules applied for the nomenklatura (inner party members), while other, more malleable rules were put in force for the average citizen.

This system began to rip apart at the seams in the 1980s, as East Germany's economy moved into yet another phase of stagnation, dissident groups and individuals began to swell, and the international environment moved decisively in favor of the West. Even still, it was all but impossible to predict East Germany's demise, and the Stasi presented a veneer of permanence in East German life. Authoritarianism can endure for decades and beyond by relying solely on oppression, and SED leaders had made recurring strategic choices to to maintain its hold on power, rather than implement economic reforms that may have improved people's circumstances. In this respect, the Stasi was only ever a partial solution to the regime's objectives.

That said, the SED leadership was not completely oblivious to the notion that it needed to reform the East German economy. Erich Honecker had pursued a policy of Kombinate, which attempted to collectivize all parts of DDR industry and manufacturing. It is likely that, against all actual evidence, Honecker and his Politburo believed this to be the path towards economic reform. Kombinate, however, was ruinous for the DDR economy and left it trailing the BRD by ever greater distances. A recession in the late 1970s, and the resulting higher interest rates charged on loans from international banks, caused another balance of payments and hard currency crisis.[109] A typical example of the priorities of the Stasi, however, were demonstrated when documents revealed that the SED had been operating a Kommerzielle Koordinierung (or KoKo for short), a secret commercial enterprise. The KoKo had almost 200 cover companies in the West that it used to smuggle hard currency back into the DDR. It is believed that KoKo generated billions of Deutsche Marks during the country's existence. Typically, the Stasi infiltrated KoKo firms, placing 19 official employees and 180 informants throughout the organization.[110] KoKo was emblematic of the DDR and the Stasi - it was corrupt, secretive and obsessed with surveillance and intelligence, rather than actually servicing the needs of the population.

Honecker

Honecker's attempts at economic reform never made much headway. Although there was an air of stability in the DDR by the 1980s, many of its citizens were deeply frustrated. It was true that the country provided a generous welfare system and that inequality was more limited compared to the West. Nevertheless, the Stasi had embedded itself deep into the real and imagined lives of East Germans. In addition, by this point, many DDR citizens could pick up West German radio and television, making them all too aware of how backwards their own state

---

[109] Ibid.
[110] Mike Dennis, *The Rise and Fall of the German Democratic Republic 1945-1990* (Harlow: Longman, 2000), p. 163.

was.

Furthermore, some East Germans were allowed to visit the West, and this again generated unrest amongst the DDR population. By the 1980s, the BRD's policy of recognition and contact, started by Willy Brandt and his Ostpolitik in the late 1960s and early 1970s, was reaping its rewards. It was a textbook case of "soft power."

As a result of the political relaxation that was taking place in the Soviet Union under Gorbachev, other regimes and dissident movements followed suit in Central and Eastern Europe. These all went further than Erich Honecker wanted. Hungarian leader János Kádár began to allow liberal economic reforms, while Poland made sudden moves to political liberalization in 1989. Polish dictator Wojciech Jaruzelski brought together opposition leaders, including the previously banned Solidarity trade union, into the so-called "Round Table" talks. The result was, stunningly, the holding of elections and the transition of power to a non-communist government.

Meanwhile, Gorbachev proclaimed that the Soviet army would no longer intervene to prop up communist regimes. At the United Nations General Assembly in December 1988, Gorbachev announced he would begin withdrawing Soviet troops from Central and Eastern Europe, and he even offered some endorsement of human rights.[111] The sand was moving from beneath the East German regime's feet, and the SED and the Stasi were now facing up to a genuinely revolutionary situation.

Markus Wolf had retired after over 30 years in charge of the HVA in 1986.[112] He spent his retirement building his own credentials as a superspy. Apparently, it was not only the capitalist Westerners who were accomplished self-promoters and marketers. Erich Mielke, on the other hand, was still in power, almost to the end of the DDR itself. The political environment changed rapidly during the 1980s, and the Stasi was suddenly faced with the resurgence of far-right sentiment. The Stasi resorted to the direct threat or use of physical violence only at the beginning and end of the DDR's existence.[113] In the 1980s, a number of dissident groups began emerging, many shielded by the church. What the authorities did not anticipate was a resurgence of German nationalism. The Stasi mounted a campaign against far right radicals after 1988 and imprisoned around 400 extreme nationalists.[114] This was a surprising turn of events, considering there had been 40 years of anti-fascist, pro-socialist propaganda. Nationalist sentiments had remained higher in the eastern part of Germany, and they were the bedrock of the far right party, Alternative für Deutschland. The Stasi kept the far right groups at bay in the 1980s, but this issue

---

[111] The Gorbachev Visit; Excerpts From Speech to U.N. on Major Soviet Military Cuts, 8 December 1988, [accessed 26 October 2017], http://www.nytimes.com/1988/12/08/world/the-gorbachev-visit-excerpts-from-speech-to-un-on-major-soviet-military-cuts.html?pagewanted=all

[112] Uwe Spiekermann (ed), 'The Stasi at Home and Abroad: Domestic Order and Foreign Intelligence', *Bulletin of the German Historical Institute*, 9 (2014), p. 20.

[113] Mary Fulbrook, *History of Germany, 1918-2000: the divided nation* (Oxford: Blackwell, 2002), p. 204.

[114] Mike Dennis, *The Rise and Fall of the German Democratic Republic 1945-1990* (Harlow: Longman, 2000), p. 207.

has clearly intensified in the years since. It was unable, however, to prevent the wave of "people power" that ultimately caused the DDR itself to integrate.

Naturally, the SED regime and its Stasi did not want rapid change. The DDR was the most recalcitrant out of all its communist peers, with the possible exception of Nicolae Ceaușescu's Romania, to reform. More than any other, the East German dictatorship knew that its very existence may be jeopardized by sudden transformation. Events, however, accelerated beyond its control in late 1989. The general atmosphere had shifted due to Gorbachev's openness and dialogue reforms, and it was also clear that the West was galloping away from the communist world in terms of material wealth. These trends had created pull factors for East Germans.

Policies in Hungary then brought this pressure to a boiling point. In the summer of 1989, Hungary started to remove its border fences with Austria. When holiday-making East Germans attempted to cross the frontier, they were unimpeded. 900 made it across.[115] Suddenly, East Germans saw their chance to leave, and thousands attempted to make the journey to freedom, through Czechoslovakia to Hungary and then Austria. Many claimed asylum in BRD embassies, including those in Prague. Honecker's regime reacted with horror and tried to stem the flow, but it could only achieve short-term pauses.

In late 1989, a refugee crisis emerged that was reminiscent of the migration of the 1950s.[116] As migrants were stopped in their tracks trying to make their way to the West, further pressure began to build in the DDR itself. Again, the focal point was the church. In the autumn of 1989 pro-reform groups began to congregate, in particular on Monday evenings at the Nikolaikirche ("Nicholas Church") in the East German city of Leipzig. After the service, they would march into the city center in a gesture of peaceful protest, demanding democratic rights. The Monday marches gathered momentum and began to concern the regime, especially as other cities mimicked the Leipzig protest.[117]

On October 7, 1989, the SED regime celebrated the 40th anniversary of the founding of the DDR with Gorbachev in attendance. Crowds in Berlin chanted the Soviet leader's name, embarrassing Honecker. Gorbachev advised the ailing leader to consider reform before it was too late.[118]

---

[115] W. Mayr, 'Hungary's Peaceful Revolution Cutting the Fence and Changing History', *Der Spiegel*, 29 May 2009, http://www.spiegel.de/international/europe/hungary-s-peaceful-revolution-cutting-the-fence-and-changing-history-a-627632.html, [accessed 31 October 2017]

[116] Norman M. Naimark, *The Russians in Germany: A History of the Soviet Zone of Occupation, 1945-1949* (Harvard: Harvard University Press, 1995), pp. 132, 133, Ferdinand Protzman, 'Jubilant East Germans Cross to West in Sealed Trains', *New York Times*, 6 October 1989, http://www.nytimes.com/1989/10/06/world/jubilant-east-germans-cross-to-west-in-sealed-trains.html, [accessed 28 October 2017]

[117] Peter Wensierski, 'Die WG der Rebellen', *Der Spiegel*, 3 October 2014, http://www.spiegel.de/einestages/leipzig-wie-es-1989-zur-montagsdemonstration-kam-a-993513.html, [accessed 31 October 2017], Mary Fulbrook, *History of Germany, 1918-2000: the divided nation* (Oxford: Blackwell, 2002), p. 264.

[118] Godfrey Hodgson, *The People's Century: From the dawn of the century to the eve of the millennium* (Godalming:

The following Monday, a further demonstration was due to be held in Leipzig. This time the Stasi were on the streets, and many feared violence and a crackdown by the authorities.[119] Fortunately, and to some surprise, the security services did not interfere in the protest. It appeared a power-struggle had taken place in the Politburo, won by reformers. Soon Honecker resigned and more liberal voices were appointed to prominent positions.[120]

More protests followed and after a botched announcement regarding travel to West Berlin, thousands gathered near the Berlin Wall on the night of November 9, 1989. Again, the security services stood down and allowed people to cross through checkpoints. That night went down in history as the moment the Berlin Wall came down, or Der Mauerfall in German. The Cold War was coming to an end, and the DDR would only survive another 11 months.[121]

After the fall of the wall, a flurry of diplomatic activity took place. BRD Chancellor Helmut Kohl saw his opportunity to reunite East Germany and West Germany, and he attempted to bring the United States, Britain, France and the Soviet Union around to his strategy. It became clear that most East German citizens favored unification, voting to power the CDU (Kohl's party) in elections in 1990, which was committed to fusion. In the end, Kohl managed to persuade friend and foe alike that a unified Germany no longer posed a threat to European peace. The East German parliament voted for unification in September 1990, paving the way for the DDR's dissolution on October 3, 1990.[122]

Within the matter of a few weeks, the Stasi had changed from guardians of the DDR's integrity to the state's biggest public enemy. Mielke was gone, and citizens began to air their grievances against the security services. Contrary to what has been claimed after the fact, the Stasi were very worried about publication of their activities. At the end of 1989 and the beginning of 1990, Stasi offices began to frantically shred documents. Berliners started to suspect that shredding was taking place and, incredibly, some citizens stormed the headquarters of the Stasi in Normannenstraße on January 15, 1990.[123] A riot ensued, and protestors occupied the offices. As a result, the issue of Stasi records entered the joint-talks and led to arrests, convictions and files made open to the public.[124] Many Stasi figures may have hoped to survive the end of the DDR, but a number of court cases were launched, including against Erich Mielke and Erich Honecker.

BBC Books, 1998), p. 592.

[119] Robert Hutchings, 'American Diplomacy and the End of the Cold War in Europe', *Foreign Policy Breakthroughs: Cases in Successful Diplomacy*, ed. Robert Hutchings and Jeremi Suri (Oxford: Oxford University Press, 2015, pp. 148-172), p. 150.

[120] Mary Fulbrook, *History of Germany, 1918-2000: the divided nation* (Oxford: Blackwell, 2002), p. 267.

[121] Robert Hutchings, 'American Diplomacy and the End of the Cold War in Europe', *Foreign Policy Breakthroughs: Cases in Successful Diplomacy*, ed. Robert Hutchings and Jeremi Suri (Oxford: Oxford University Press, 2015, pp. 148-172), p. 161.

[122] "Politics in Germany: The Online Edition", University of California, Irvine, [accessed 30 October 2017], http://www.socsci.uci.edu/~rdalton/germany/ch2/chap2.htm

[123] Mike Dennis, *The Rise and Fall of the German Democratic Republic 1945-1990* (Harlow: Longman, 2000), p. 292.

[124] Peter Pulzer, *German Politics, 1945-1995* (Oxford: Oxford University Press, 1995), p. 158

The former was "only" convicted of his 1930s murders, and Honecker fled to Chile.

Even more controversially, the unified Federal Republic of Germany opened the Stasi files in 1992. The results shocked the world. The files stretched to 178 kilometers worth of material.[125] They showed that at one point the Stasi had one informant per 6.5 East German citizens.[126] Almost a third of East German citizens had some record of surveillance material filed on them. The shock of the extent of Stasi spying, and the scope of collaboration, cast a long shadow over East German society, even as it became absorbed into the new capitalist Federal Republic. As German historian Hubertus Knabe put it, "But why did the Stasi collect all this information in its archives? The main purpose was to control the society. In nearly every speech, the Stasi minister gave the order to find out who is who, which meant who thinks what. He didn't want to wait until somebody tried to act against the regime. He wanted to know in advance what people were thinking and planning. The East Germans knew, of course, that they were surrounded by informers, in a totalitarian regime that created mistrust and a state of widespread fear, the most important tools to oppress people in any dictatorship."

Perhaps surprisingly, the memory of both the Stasi and the DDR state is contested in modern German society. Gradually, there has been an advent of Ostalgie, nostalgia for the old days in the East (Ost). Easterners, many of whom lost their jobs in the 1990s as industry was either closed or moved to the West, have been unhappy with the new status quo. Western Germans have derided Easterners as "Ossis," and former DDR inhabitants believe they are treated as second-class citizens. This has also affected anti-immigrant sentiment in the East, which produced the 1992 riots in Rostock.

Westerners, in Germany and beyond, have caricatured the DDR as a "Stasi State" of deep-seated and insidious surveillance by an immoral and corrupt security apparatus. Memorials have been set up around the former DDR to commemorate the victims and practices of the Stasi, for instance at the Hohenschönhausen prison. In the 1990s, regular scandals appeared from the former DDR, especially those concerning the Stasi. Films such as *Das Leben der Anderen* have exacerbated this trend, but in the end, most Stasi operatives and agents were essentially pardoned during the 1990s.[127] Of course, that did not prevent many high profile figures, such as Christa Wolf and many active politicians, of being accused of collaboration with the Stasi.[128]

Nevertheless, a great deal of resentment exists in the eastern portion of modern Germany. Former Stasi agents have taken exception to their portrayal in museums and in the press,

---

[125] David Bathrick, 'Memories and Fantasies About and By the Stasi', in: David Clarke, Ute Wölfel (eds), *Remembering the German Democratic Republic: Divided Memory in a United Germany* (Basingstoke: Palgrave Macmillan, 2011, pp. 223-234), p. 223.
[126] Paul H Robinson, Sarah M. Robinson, *Pirates, Prisoners, and Lepers: Lessons from Life Outside the Law*, (University of Nebraska Press, 2015), p. 156.
[127] Doris M. Epler, *The Berlin Wall: How it Rose and Why it Fell* (Brookfield: The Millbrook Press, 1992), p. 110.
[128] Nick Hodgin, 'Screening the Stasi', ed. N. Hodgin and C. Pearce, *The GDR Remembered: Representations of the East German State since 1989* (Camden House, 2011, pp. 69-91), p. 74.

claiming they were acting within the law of the times.[129] Some have even expressed pride in their work.[130] Furthermore, some former citizens of the DDR have, over time, remembered with pride the social welfare available in their state, and they have downplayed the role of the Stasi.[131] This is the core feature of Ostalgie.

Even as some in the former East Germany cling to an idealized past, a closer look at the history of the Stasi reveals the unique penetration the security services achieved in the lives of everyday citizens. Both at home and abroad, the Stasi proved itself to be a highly effective spying agency. At home, it created a uniquely stifling atmosphere of paranoia and frustration, and it managed to obtain information abroad that consistently embarrassed Western governments. All the while, the Stasi was used to paper over the cracks of an ineffectual authoritarian regime whose survival proved to be contingent on the Cold War. The Stasi could not extend the life of the SED regime beyond the end of that conflict, nor could it stop the ultimate rebellion of a people desperate for more freedom.

Online Resources

Other books about Russian history by Charles River Editors

Other books about East German history by Charles River Editors

Other books about the Stasi on Amazon

Other books about the KGB operations on Amazon

Further Reading about the KGB

Abramov I. (2006) Counterintelligence. Shield and sword against the Abwehr and the CIA. Moscow.

Archive of the Cheka. Collection of documents, (2007) edited by Vinogradov V., Litvin A., Khristoforov V. Moscow. Kuchkovo Pole.

Collins, E. (1998) Myth, Manifesto, Meltdown: Communist Strategy, 1848-1991. Praeger

Gordievskiy, O. & Andru, Q. (1992) History of foreign policy operations from Lenin to Gorbachev. Moscow. Available at https://www.e-reading.club/book.php?book=15654

---

[129] Sara Jones, 'At Home With the Stasi', In: David Clarke, Ute Wölfel (eds), *Remembering the German Democratic Republic: Divided Memory in a United Germany* (Basingstoke: Palgrave Macmillan, 2011, pp. 211-222), p. 221.

[130] David Bathrick, 'Memories and Fantasies About and By the Stasi', in: David Clarke, Ute Wölfel (eds), *Remembering the German Democratic Republic: Divided Memory in a United Germany* (Basingstoke: Palgrave Macmillan, 2011, pp. 223-234), p. 234.

[131] Sara Jones, 'At Home With the Stasi', In: David Clarke, Ute Wölfel (eds), *Remembering the German Democratic Republic: Divided Memory in a United Germany* (Basingstoke: Palgrave Macmillan, 2011, pp. 211-222), p. 221.

Khlobustov, O. (2017) KGB of the USSR 1954-1991. The secrets of the collapse of Great Power. Moscow

Lubyanka: Organs of the Cheka-OGPU-NKVD-MGB-MVD-KGB. 1917-1991. (2003) Moscow

Mlechin, L. (2017) KGB. Presidents of the state security bodies. Declassified Fates. Moscow

Sever, A. (2008) History of KGB. Moscow: Algorithm - Shield and sword. Available at https://www.e-reading.club/bookreader.php/147187/Sever_-_Istoriya_KGB.html

Shevyakin A.P. (2004) Security System of the USSR (1945-1991). Structures. Leadership. Moscow.

Simbirdzev, I. (2017) Cheka in Leninist Russia. 1917-1922: In the glow of the revolution.

Further Reading about the Stasi

Gary Bruce, *Resistance with the people: repression and resistance in Eastern Germany, 1945 – 1955* (Oxford: Rowman & Littlefield, 2003)

University of California, "Politics in Germany: The Online Edition", University of California, Irvine, [accessed 30 October 2017], http://www.socsci.uci.edu/~rdalton/germany/ch2/chap2.htm

David Childs and Richard Popplewell, *The Stasi: The East German Intelligence and Security Service* (New York: New York University Press, 1996)

David Clarke, Ute Wölfel (eds), *Remembering the German Democratic Republic: Divided Memory in a United Germany* (Basingstoke: Palgrave Macmillan, 2011)

David Crossland, 'Dynamo Berlin: The soccer club 'owned' by the Stasi', *CNN*, 14 January 2016, http://edition.cnn.com/2016/01/13/football/dynamo-berlin-stasi-east-germany-football/index.html

Mike Dennis, *The Rise and Fall of the German Democratic Republic 1945-1990* (Harlow: Longman, 2000)

Deutsche Welle, "The legacy of the 1977 German Autumn of left-wing terror", 5 September 2017, http://www.dw.com/en/the-legacy-of-the-1977-german-autumn-of-left-wing-terror/a-40365602 [accessed 17 January 2018]

Deutsche Welle, "Africa and communist East Germany", [accessed 18 October 2017], http://www.dw.com/en/africa-and-communist-east-germany/g-18753769

Rainer Eckert, 'Flächendeckender Überwachung', *Der Spiegel*, 1 January 1993, http://www.spiegel.de/spiegel/spiegelspecial/d-55475506.html

Andrew Evans, "The Last Gasp of Socialism: Economics and Culture in 1960s East Germany", *German Life and Letters*, (63, 2010, pp. 331–344)

Anna Funder, *Stasiland: Stories From Behind the Berlin Wall* (London: Granta, 2003)

William Glenn Gray, *Germany's Cold War: The Global Campaign to Isolate East Germany, 1949-1969* (London: University of North Carolina Press, 2003)

Godfrey Hodgson, *The People's Century: From the dawn of the century to the eve of the millennium* (Godalming: BBC Books, 1998)

Niall Ferguson, *Kissinger 1923-1968: The Idealist* (London: Allen Lane, 2015)

Mary Fulbrook, *History of Germany, 1918-2000: the divided nation* (Oxford: Blackwell, 2002)

Jeffrey Herf, 'East Germany's Assault on Israel', *Commentary Magazine*, 16 May 2016, https://www.commentarymagazine.com/articles/east-germanys-assault-israel/, [accessed 11 January 2018]

Nick Hodgin, 'Screening the Stasi', ed. N. Hodgin and C. Pearce, *The GDR Remembered: Representations of the East German State since 1989* (Camden House, 2011, pp. 69-91)

Robert Hutchings, 'American Diplomacy and the End of the Cold War in Europe', *Foreign Policy Breakthroughs: Cases in Successful Diplomacy*, ed. Robert Hutchings and Jeremi Suri (Oxford: Oxford University Press, 2015, pp. 148-172)

Konrad H. Jarausch and Helga A. Welsh, "Two Germanies, 1961-1989", German History in Documents and Images (German Historical Institute: http://germanhistorydocs.ghi-dc.org/, [accessed 6 October 2017]

W. Mayr, 'Hungary's Peaceful Revolution Cutting the Fence and Changing History', *Der Spiegel*, 29 May 2009, http://www.spiegel.de/international/europe/hungary-s-peaceful-revolution-cutting-the-fence-and-changing-history-a-627632.html, [accessed 31 October 2017]

Norman M. Naimark, *The Russians in Germany: A History of the Soviet Zone of Occupation, 1945-1949* (Harvard: Harvard University Press, 1995)

The Gorbachev Visit; Excerpts From Speech to U.N. on Major Soviet Military Cuts, *New York Times*, 8 December 1988, [accessed 26 October 2017], http://www.nytimes.com/1988/12/08/world/the-gorbachev-visit-excerpts-from-speech-to-un-on-major-soviet-military-cuts.html?pagewanted=all

Thomas Parrish, *Berlin in the balance, 1945 - 1949: the blockade, the airlift, the first mayor battle of the Cold War* (Reading: Addison Wesley, 1998)

Patrick Pesnot, Great Spies of the 20th Century, (Barnsley: Pen & Sword Military, 2016)

Ferdinand Protzman, 'Jubilant East Germans Cross to West in Sealed Trains', *New York Times*, 6 October 1989, http://www.nytimes.com/1989/10/06/world/jubilant-east-germans-cross-to-west-in-sealed-trains.html, [accessed 28 October 2017]

Peter Pulzer, *German Politics, 1945-1995* (Oxford: Oxford University Press, 1995)

Paul H Robinson, Sarah M. Robinson, *Pirates, Prisoners, and Lepers: Lessons from Life Outside the Law*, (University of Nebraska Press, 2015)

M.E. Sarotte, *Dealing with the Devil: East Germany, Detente, and Ostpolitik, 1969-1973*, (The University of North Carolina Press, 2001)

John R. Schindler, 'This Mass Murder Mystery Has Terrorism, Spies, Palestinians, Stasi and the FBI', *Observer*, 16 September 2016, http://observer.com/2016/09/this-mass-murder-mystery-has-terrorism-spies-palestinians-stasi-and-the-fbi/

Uwe Spiekermann (ed), 'The Stasi at Home and Abroad: Domestic Order and Foreign Intelligence', *Bulletin of the German Historical Institute*, 9 (2014)

'Stasi Prison', Gedenkstätte Berlin-Hohenschönhausen, [accessed 5 January 2018], http://www.stiftung-hsh.de/history/stasi-prison/

Henry Thomson, "Repression, Redistribution and the Problem of Authoritarian Control", *East European Politics and Societies*, (31: 1, 2017, pp. 68 – 92)

Lally Weymouth, East Germany's Dirty Secret, *The Washington Post*, 14 October 1990, https://www.washingtonpost.com/archive/opinions/1990/10/14/east-germanys-dirty-secret/09375b6f-2ae1-4173-a0dc-77a9c276aa4b/?utm_term=.56b13dbc821c

Peter Wensierski, 'Die WG der Rebellen', *Der Spiegel*, 3 October 2014, http://www.spiegel.de/einestages/leipzig-wie-es-1989-zur-montagsdemonstration-kam-a-993513.html, [accessed 31 October 2017]

Gareth M. Winrow, *The Foreign Policy of the GDR in Africa* (Cambridge: Cambridge University Press, 1990)

Gregory R. Witkowski, "Peasants Revolt? Re-evaluating the 17 June Uprising in East Germany", *German History*, (24:2, 1 April 2006, pp. 243–266)

Free Books by Charles River Editors

We have brand new titles available for free most days of the week. To see which of our titles are currently free, click on this link.

Discounted Books by Charles River Editors

We have titles at a discount price of just 99 cents everyday. To see which of our titles are currently 99 cents, click on this link.

Made in the USA
Monee, IL
09 March 2022

92555465R00063